• Oxford University Press •

GALLERY

• Paula Fassman Suzanne Tavares •

Oxford University Press

200 Madison Avenue
New York, N.Y. 10016 USA

Walton Street
Oxford OX2 6DP England

OXFORD is a trademark of Oxford University Press.

Library of Congress Cataloging-in-Publication
Data
(Revised for vol. 1)

Fassman, Paula.
Gallery.

Rev. ed. of: Gallery. 1982.
1. English language—Study and teaching—
Foreign speakers. I. Tavares, Suzanne Seymour.
II. Fassman, Paula. Gallery. III. Title.
PE1128.A2F29 1989 428.2′4 88-36851
ISBN 0-19-434279-4

Cover design by April Okano.

Illustrations by Daniel Abraham, Don Brown, Kerry Gavin and Karin Kretschmann. Graphics by Joseph DePinho, Maj-Britt Hagsted, Sarah Sills and Stephan Van Litsenborg.

Printing (last digit): 10 9 8 7 6 5 4 3 2 1

Printed in Hong Kong.

Acknowledgments

We would like to thank all our friends and colleagues at the American Language Institute in Lisbon, Portugal, who showed an interest in this project. Thank you also to Mary Lynne, Jeannie, April, Debbie and the rest of the team at OUP for their encouragement and support. As always, a special thanks to Jorge, David, Paul and Al for their invaluable moral support.

Contents

Introduction

Gallery 1 is an upper beginning-level text for adults and young adults learning English as a second or foreign language. It was written specifically to meet the needs of lower-level students who will be going into Gallery 2, and like Gallery 2, provides material for 60 to 120 hours of instruction, depending on the design of your program and the time allotted to each level.

Each unit focuses on one or more structural and functional areas of high priority to lower level students. The functions were carefully chosen to provide beginning students with the life and survival skills they will need as beginners who are trying to "get around" in English. The structures presented are those that serve as building blocks leading to communication and fluency.

A complete integrated-skills coursebook, Gallery 1 features 10 chapters, each containing a variety of activities which provide practice in listening, speaking, reading, and writing. These activities were designed not only to interest, but to challenge and motivate adult beginners.

Interesting contexts provide the student with exposure to the language focus of each unit. Then, through a carefully-staged series of both communicative and guided activities, students gain confidence and skill in using the language. The topics and language areas in Gallery 1 were carefully chosen with students' real communicative needs in mind. When students perceive language as relevant and potentially useful to them in real life, their motivation to learn increases, as well as their investment and involvement in the learning process.

PEDAGOGICAL ORIENTATION

COMMUNICATIVE PRACTICE

All too often, teachers avoid communicative practice at the lower levels, assuming that students are only "equipped" to speak in guided situations. The fact is that even beginners need to be given an opportunity to work on their communicative competence. Improvising, "trying out," paraphrasing, etc. are communication strategies that all language users need to develop—even though students' grasp of the mechanics of the language may be limited at the beginning levels. Communicative teaching and learning allow the student to learn in a more natural way, make the classroom experience more student-centered and ensure a high degree of learner involvement. As students become more proficient, language rules are gradually worked out. Gallery 1 features activities in which students initiate language and say things that are relevant and meaningful to them.

GUIDED PRACTICE

If learning takes place naturally, is it a good idea to give students structure practice and guided activities? Most students need to practice the language in more organized and formal contexts as long as these contexts are interesting and not mechanical. Controlled practice, which is cognitive and which reflects natural language use, is an anchor for students and allows them to see how the language is organized. Gallery 1 also features activities that allow for this type of learning at various points throughout each unit.

ORGANIZATION OF THE BOOK

Each unit opens with a Presentation section, which is the students' first exposure to the language focus of the chapter. In this section, an interesting context is presented, which illustrates, in a natural way, how and when the language is used. An Input section gives the student an even broader view of how the language works. Through a variety of authentic-sounding listenings, which include everything from humorous and thought-provoking dialogues to radio shows and tourist information, students get a chance to see how the featured language areas function in a variety of ways. A Language Summary clearly maps out how and when the target structures and functions are used. An Intensive Practice section gives students controlled to less-controlled practice through cognitive drills that highlight accuracy. Reading sections, which include pre- and post-reading activities, offer students a diverse range of topics—all of high interest to the adult learner. A Writing section provides an opportunity for in-class writing practice or homework. The activities are carefully developed to make the writing experience a motivating, not frustrating one for the beginning learner who has not had much experience in writing techniques. Through this series of free and controlled activities, students get a chance to work on fluency AND accuracy, the two fundamental aspects of language proficiency.

A textbook cannot be all things to all people, but it should be flexible enough to suit every teaching style and the needs of many different types of students. With this in mind, the sections in each unit of Gallery 1 have been designed to be modular. That is, teachers should feel free to change their order, stress one section over another, and even leave out a section if it is not useful or relevant to a teaching situation. The objectives of each class will be different, and Gallery 1 should be adapted so that these objectives can best be met.

HOW TO USE EACH SECTION

PRESENTATION

This section sets up a context where students are subtly introduced to the structures and/or functions that will be the focus of the unit. The tasks in this section give students an opportunity to start working communicatively with the language. Books for lower level students often assume that learners know absolutely nothing about the language or subject at hand, an assumption that can often be discouraging for students. The Presentation section in Gallery 1 always provides brainstorming activities so that students can demonstrate, right away, what they already know. This is a good diagnostic tool for the teacher, who can then decide how thoroughly the different language points in the unit should be dealt with. Brainstorming may also spark interest in the topic and often encourages students to communicate with each other. Giving the students a chance to share what they already know through brainstorming functions as a peer-teaching technique, and is an all-important feature of the Presentation section.

Since the purpose of the Presentation is to introduce the language in the unit, provide a diagnostic tool for the teacher, and allow for peer-sharing opportunities, the emphasis should be on fluency and communication. Therefore, it is advisable to hold back on serious correction until further sections. Gentle guidance toward accuracy is the key.

INPUT

In this section students receive more exposure to the language focus of the unit and knowledge of how it works, through a variety of interesting listening selections. Each selection is preceded by Warm-Up activities that get students thinking about the topic of the unit before they actually perform any specific tasks. Warm-Up activities are varied (predicting, brainstorming, fact sharing, etc.) and, in many cases, introduce subject matter and vocabulary that are essential for comprehension of the listening segment. Once the students' interest in the topic has been awakened, they are given a global task to check their overall grasp of meaning and then a more specific task so that they can work with the language in more detail.

LANGUAGE SUMMARY

This section includes a summary of the forms and usage of the target structures and functions of the unit. This section also marks a break in the unit, introducing the more structured or controlled exercises. Though this was designed for at-home use or to guide teachers to the target structures of each unit, some students may want to refer to it in class, or go over it before the Intensive Practice to make sure they understand the forms and usages. In either case it is provided within each unit as a reference or a checklist for student and teacher use.

INTENSIVE PRACTICE

By this time, students have had ample practice with the target structures and functions in rather open-ended communicative types of activities. Intensive Practice activities involve a more structured practice of the grammatical form. In this section of the unit, the focus is more on form—or accuracy—than on fluency. However, the exercises are designed to be cognitive and to allow for creative input on the part of the students, while still giving them valuable practice in dealing with the grammar or functional focus of the unit in more controlled contexts. There is a variety of exercise types in this section, all designed to elicit the target structures and functions in different contexts. They can be done either as oral or written activities. As has been said before, the sections of the unit do not have to be done in order; many of the exercises in this section of the unit can be handled nicely in the beginning of class, giving the students the control they may want before they are "warmed up." One way to make these exercises work as quick oral drills is to place the cue words on flashcards; in many cases leaving off the verb forms will make it more challenging to the students. Many Intensive Practice exercises make interesting role plays, and the teacher should feel free to expand the exercises as long as the structures and functions are used correctly.

READING

Reading is an excellent source of input, a great vehicle for vocabulary building and gives students a tremendous feeling of satisfaction and achievement. Even beginning students can read at a fairly high level of proficiency, which enables us to take advantage of a wide range of interesting topics. Gallery 1 readings, though graded to be accessible to the lower level student, focus on such adult topics as—the European Common Market, tourism, famous people, consumer awareness, and others that involve personal and social themes. Each reading is preceded by a pre-reading exercise which explores the students' knowledge of the theme and vocabulary, and allows them to share thoughts and ideas. Post-reading exercises, besides acting as comprehension checks, offer students more opportunities to talk about the subject. We suggest that you allow students to read silently at their own pace and never aloud before the whole class. Students may come up against new vocabulary that wasn't dealt with in the pre-reading phase. When this happens, it is a good idea to encourage them to figure out the meaning from context, a strategy that all readers should learn to develop.

WRITING

In this section, students begin to develop writing skills through a series of free and controlled activities. Students begin by reading or talking about a topic and then work on a related writing task, either in class or at home. Many times, models are given so students do not feel frustrated at the prospect of putting pen to paper without direction. It should often be stressed that writing is a communicative process and that communication is the goal. Students can be given other opportunities to write throughout the unit and should be encouraged to develop their writing skills whenever possible.

A FEW FINAL WORDS

The material in Gallery 1 is the product of actual lesson material used successfully in classes. However, every teacher has his/her own teaching style and special relationship with different groups of students with different kinds of needs. That is why, as teachers, we would like to suggest that you always feel free to adapt the book to your own teaching style and the needs of your students.

And finally, though each of the chapters of the book uses a language point as its anchor, it is very important to remember that the free conversational opportunities offered by the material are of at least equal importance if a balance between fluency and accuracy is to be achieved.

1 Tell me something about yourself.

PRESENTATION

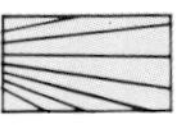

A. Look at the three pictures below. The first one illustrates *work,* the second *family,* and the third *studies.* What questions can you ask someone about each of these categories? Working with your classmates, think of as many questions as you can.

B. Choose two or three questions from each category. Make a questionnaire like the one below on another sheet of paper and write your questions on it.

	Class Questionnaire	
	1.	4.
	2.	5.
	3.	6.

C. Now ask one of your classmates the questions on your list. Take notes on the answers and report to the class what you found out.

A. Look at the pictures. What do you think these people are like? Are they single or married? Do they live alone? Do they like what they are doing? Working with one or two of your classmates, use your imagination and write a description of each person.

B. Now listen to interviews with the people in the pictures and see if you were right.

Working with a partner, practice asking and answering questions about the people using the information in the interviews.

INPUT

What kind of work do these women do? What do you think their jobs are like? Discuss your answers with your classmates.

A. Listen to an interview. Does the woman speaking do any of the jobs in the pictures?

B. Listen again. What does the woman like about her job? What doesn't she like? Make a form like the one below on another sheet of paper and take notes on it as you listen. Then compare your notes with those of your classmates.

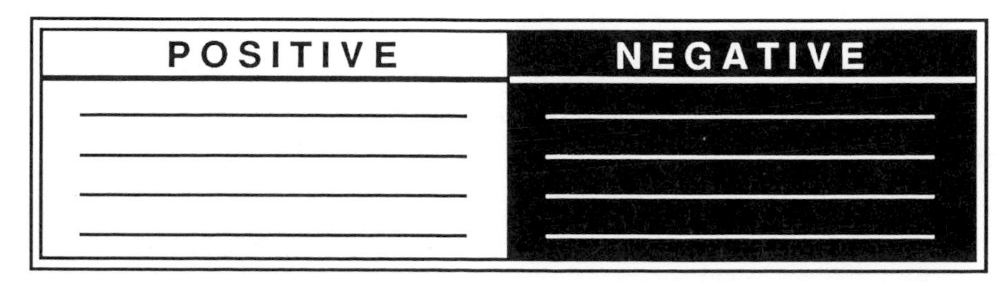

LANGUAGE SUMMARY

Asking For and Giving Personal Information

FUNCTIONS

- Asking for information about work:

What do you do?
What does your sister do?
Do you like working in an office?

- Asking for information about families:

Are you married?
How many children do you have?
How many brothers and sisters do you have?

- Asking for personal information:

Where do you live?
Do you like living alone?
Does your brother go to school?

- Giving information about work:

I'm an engineer.
I'm an executive in the sales department of a large insurance company.

- Giving information about families:

I'm married and I have two children, a boy and a girl.
I have three brothers and one sister.

- Giving personal information:

I'm a college student.
I like living in New York.

STRUCTURES

- Present tense of *be:*

I'm He's She's	a computer programmer.	Are you Is he Is she	a student?

- Present tense:

I live He lives She lives	in Miami.	Where	do you does he does she	work?

- The *-ing* form of the verb with *like:*

I	like don't like	living in New York.

Does he like	studying French? living with a roommate? working for IBM?

INTENSIVE PRACTICE

A

Working with a partner, give a negative statement with *like* that matches each of the following. Use the example as a guide.

John's a car salesman.
Yes, but he doesn't like selling cars.

1. Fred and Barbara are law students.
2. Martha's an English teacher.
3. Yvonne is a dress designer.
4. Pete is an office worker.
5. Jim and Robert are TV repairmen.
6. Paul is a basketball player.

B

Here are two forms filled out by people applying for a job. Working with a partner, use the information in the forms to ask and answer questions about these people. Use the example as a guide.

STUDENT A: *What's this person's name?*
STUDENT B: *Steven Gimble.*

STUDENT B: *Where does Elaine Bennet live?*
STUDENT A: *She lives in Brooklyn.*

Application for Employment

PERSONAL INFORMATION

NAME (last, first, middle)
Gimble, Steven R.

SOCIAL SECURITY NUMBER
264-72-4190

ADDRESS (street, city, state, zip code)
4727 Harrison St, Hollywood, Florida 33131

TELEPHONE NUMBER
(305) 555-9911
Area Code

Are you a U.S. citizen? yes

If not, do you have the legal right to remain permanently in the United States? ______

Employment History

Month/Year	Name/Address of Employer	Salary	Position
From 6/85 To 9/86	Deltronix Company 76 Smith St. Miami, Florida	$18,000	Electronic Technician
From 11/86 To Present	Marlis Engineering Industries Bay Parkway Hollywood, Florida	$23,000	Junior Engineer

Employment Application

Name Bennet (last) Elaine (first) Sarah (middle)

Address 9727 75th St. (street) Brooklyn (city) NY (state) 11209 (zip)

Phone (718) (area code) 555-6477

Are you a U.S. citizen? yes

If not, do you have the legal right to remain permanently in the United States? ______

Education

Name and Location	From Month/Year	To Month/Year	Degrees Earned
High School: Roosevelt High School, Hyde Park, NY	9/80	6/84	Diploma
College: Indiana University, Bloomington, IN	9/84	5/88	B.A. European History

C

Look at the pictures and then talk about this man and his family with your classmates. For example, you might begin like this:

1.

He's probably 45 or 50 years old, he sells used cars for East Los Angeles Car Sales . . .

2.

3.

4.

5.

6.

READING

A You are going to read a text in which the following words and phrases appear: *taste, college degree, flavors, odorless, spit out,* and *sample.* Use one of these words or phrases to complete each of the following sentences.

1. There are many different ________ of ice cream—chocolate, vanilla, strawberry, etc.
2. When the little boy put a stone in his mouth, his mother said, " ________ it ________, or you might swallow it!"
3. Could you ________ this lemonade to see if it needs more sugar?
4. The salesman gave me a small ________ of his product to try out.
5. When a person finishes college, he or she receives a ________.
6. Water, when it is pure, has no smell or odor. It is ________.

B Do you know anyone who has an unusual job? Discuss it with your classmates. Then read the text below to find out about another unusual job.

What Does a Chocolate Taster Do?

Everybody loves chocolate. But did you know that some people have jobs as chocolate tasters? They work for candy companies and get paid to taste chocolate. It sounds like the best job in the world—and the easiest.

Perhaps it is fun, but it is not easy. A chocolate taster must have many years of training. A chocolate taster needs a college degree in food science, chemistry, or biochemistry.

The chocolate taster doesn't work alone. Several tasters sit at a round table in an air-conditioned, odorless room with samples of the products in front of them.

The tasters do not speak to each other while they work. Instead, they take notes. Later the group discusses the "good" and "bad" flavors they taste. Chocolate tasters do not get fat, because they usually spit out the product, and they only taste a very small amount.

Chocolate tasting is an important job. The quality of the product depends on the chocolate taster's skill. Think of that the next time you eat a chocolate bar.

All of the following statements are false. Read the text again and correct the statements. When correcting the statements, give more information. Use the example as a guide.

A chocolate taster's job is easy.
No, a chocolate taster's job is not easy. He or she needs a college degree in chemistry, food science, or biochemistry and usually has a long training period.

1. A chocolate taster usually works alone.
2. Chocolate tasters often get fat.
3. Chocolate tasters speak to each other as they work.
4. A chocolate taster's job is not very important.

WRITING

Read the description of Abel Machado. Then interview a classmate and write a similar description of him or her.

Abel Machado is a flight engineer, and he works for Iberia Airlines. He's from Caceres, Spain, but he lives and works in Madrid. He is married and he has two children, a daughter, Mercedes, and a son, Carlos.

2 Excuse me, does this bus go to Riverdale?

PRESENTATION

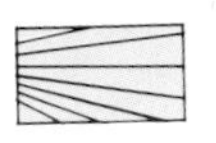

When we are traveling in new places, we often need to ask questions. Imagine that you are in the places shown below. Working with your classmates, decide questions you might need to ask.

A train station in London. You want to go to Oxford.

A New York bus stop. You want to go to the Metropolitan Museum of Art.

A bus station in Montreal, Canada. You want to take a bus to the city of Ottawa.

A city where you've never been before.

Now listen to tourists in these situations asking for help. See if any of your questions are asked. Do the tourists in the conversations have any problems?

Tell the class some useful facts about transportation in a city you know well. What kinds of public transportation does the city have? How do you pay for it? What are its problems?

Useful Vocabulary
bus, subway, cheap, expensive, fast, efficient, crowded, ticket, driver, exact change

INPUT

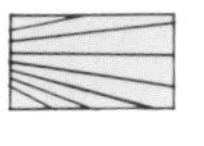

Frank and Liz are in Paris, and they want to see Napoleon's Tomb. Look at the pictures. Working with your classmates, decide what questions Frank and Liz are probably asking.

A. Listen to the conversation between Frank and Liz. Then decide what order the pictures above should be put in.

B. Listen again and make a list of all the questions that Frank asks. How do they compare with the ones you and your classmates thought of?

LANGUAGE SUMMARY

Asking For and Giving Directions

FUNCTIONS

- Asking about transportation:

When is the next train to Ottawa?
What platform does it leave from?
How much does it cost?
Does this train go to Oxford?
Could you tell us when we get there, please?

- Asking for directions:

We're looking for Taft Street.
How far is it to Main Street?
What's a good place to eat around here?
Where can I get some stamps?

- Giving locations:

There's one on Market Street.
There's one across from the park.

STRUCTURES

- Present tense:

Do I have to change buses?
Does this bus go downtown?
What time does the 6:00 train get into Montreal?

- *Be:*

Is it far to Market Street?
How much is a one-way ticket to Hartford?
Where is the nearest bank?

- *Could you* for polite requests:

Could you give me a ticket, please?
Could you tell me what time it is?

- *There is:*

There's	a tourist office	on 47th Street.
	one	

Excuse me, is there a souvenir shop near here?

INTENSIVE PRACTICE

A

Here are two ways to ask where things are:

Excuse me, is there a _________ near here?
Excuse me, where's the nearest _________?

Use each of these ways to ask about the following:

1. post office
2. bank
3. tourist office
4. subway station
5. drugstore
6. souvenir shop

B

Now work with a partner. Student A, ask questions like those in exercise A. Student B, give answers based on the map below. Use the example as a guide.

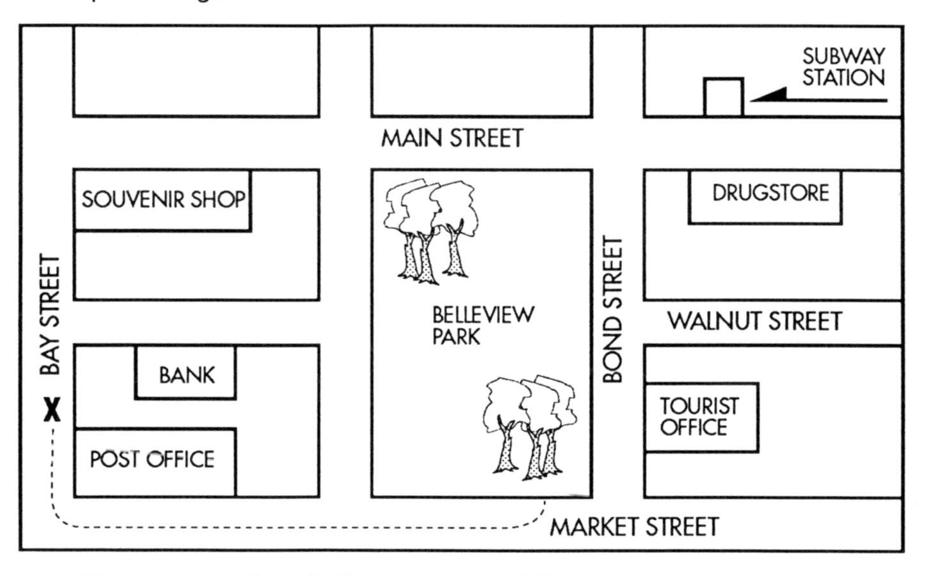

A: *Excuse me, where's the nearest park?*

B: *There's one on* Market *Street.*

Now look at the map again. Suppose you and your partner are standing at X. Student B, ask how to get to each of the numbered places. Student A, answer in one of the following ways:

There's one	*across the street.*
	two blocks down.
	around the corner.
	across from the park.
	on Main Street.

D

Working with a partner, use the following cues to have a conversation. A, you are a tourist. B, you are a ticket agent.

A: Ask about the next train to Hartford.
B: Answer: 6:30.
A: Ask about the price of a round-trip ticket.
B: Answer: $15.75.
A: Ask about changing trains.
B: Answer: no—direct.
A: Ask what time the train gets into Hartford.
B: Answer: 8:45.
A: Ask about the platform.
B: Answer: platform B.
A: Thank your partner.
B: Answer.

E

Tourists often need to buy things when they are traveling. Practice asking questions. Use the example as a guide.

Excuse me, where can I get	*a snack* *some stamps*	*around here?*

F

Read the useful phrases on the left. Then cover them up and practice with a partner using only the cues on the right.

Excuse me, . . .

1.	. . . I'm looking for Main Street.	Look/Main St.
2.	. . . what's a good place to eat around here?	Eat
3.	. . . where can I cash traveler's checks?	Traveler's Checks
4.	. . . is it far to Market Street?	Far/Market St.
5.	. . . does this bus go to Riverdale?	This Bus/Riverdale
6.	. . . how much is it to Belleview Park?	How much/Belleview Park
7.	. . . do I need exact change?	Exact change
8.	. . . do I have to change buses/trains?	Change | Buses Trains

READING

A You are going to read an article about tourists. Work with a partner and write five words related to travel and tourists, such as *ticket, visit,* and *airplane.* When you finish, share your words with the rest of the class.

B Read the text below. Do any of the words that you thought of appear in it?

The Trouble With Tourists Is . . .

Some tourists know very little about geography. Often they do not even know the capital of the country they are visiting. They want to drive in Venice, they think Lisbon is in Spain, and they are sure that every mountain in Switzerland is the Matterhorn.

"Some tourists give us headaches," said one tour guide. "They complain about the food and the hotels. Or they leave the group to buy a souvenir or have a cup of coffee and then miss the bus." When this happens, the bus waits for half an hour and then leaves without them. It is their responsibility to find the group again.

"Because they are not always careful," explains Albano Gomes of the Sines Tour Agency, "tourists are often the victims of robbery. The tour guide sometimes has to spend hours at the police station. The rest of the people on the tour have to wait for another guide." But tourists are very welcome in the countries they visit. Italy, a country of 56 million inhabitants, receives about 48 million tourists a year who contribute over $8 billion to the Italian economy. In the Bahamas, approximately 70% of the country's revenue comes from tourism. And tourists help us understand the customs of the countries they come from. So most people agree that tourists are important—even if they think that Bern is the capital of Germany.

C Use the information in the text to talk about the following picture.

WRITING

Look at this page from a tourist brochure. It gives some useful information about Lisbon, Portugal. Using the page as a guide, write similar information about your city.

Helpful Hints — Getting Around in Lisbon

Banks and Money Exchange

Banks are open from 8:30 A.M. to 11:45 A.M. and from 1:00 to 2:45 P.M. They are closed on Saturdays and Sundays. However, you can exchange foreign currency at the airport and the main train station every day of the week until 11:00 P.M.

Portugese Currency

The Portuguese monetary unit is the *escudo.* The symbol for the escudo is $, the same as the dollar sign.

Pharmacies

The word for pharmacy in Portuguese is *farmacia.* Pharmacies in Lisbon are open from 9:00 A.M. to 1:00 P.M. and from 3:00 P.M. to 7:00 P.M. If you need to buy something at a time when most pharmacies are closed, you can do so at a *farmacia de servico* — pharmacies that stay open 24 hours a day.

First Aid

In case of emergency or if you need first aid, go to the Santa Maria University Hospital on Av. Professor Egaz Moniz. This hospital has a modern cardiology unit and a large emergency ward.

Postal Services

The main Post Office (called *correio*) in the Praca dos Restauradores is open 24 hours a day.

Shopping

Lisbon's main shopping district is the downtown area, called the *Baixa.* The Avenida da Roma in the uptown district also has many fine shops. Stores are usually open from 9:00 A.M. to 1:00 P.M. and from 3:00 P.M. to 7:00 P.M. The Commercial Center Amoreiras, near the Marques de Pombal, is one of Europe's largest shopping centers. It has over 300 shops and restaurants and is open from 10:00 A.M. to 12 midnight every day.

3 Tell me about your country.

PRESENTATION

A. Look at the symbols and the map of the world. Can you match each symbol with a country? Some symbols may go with more than one country.

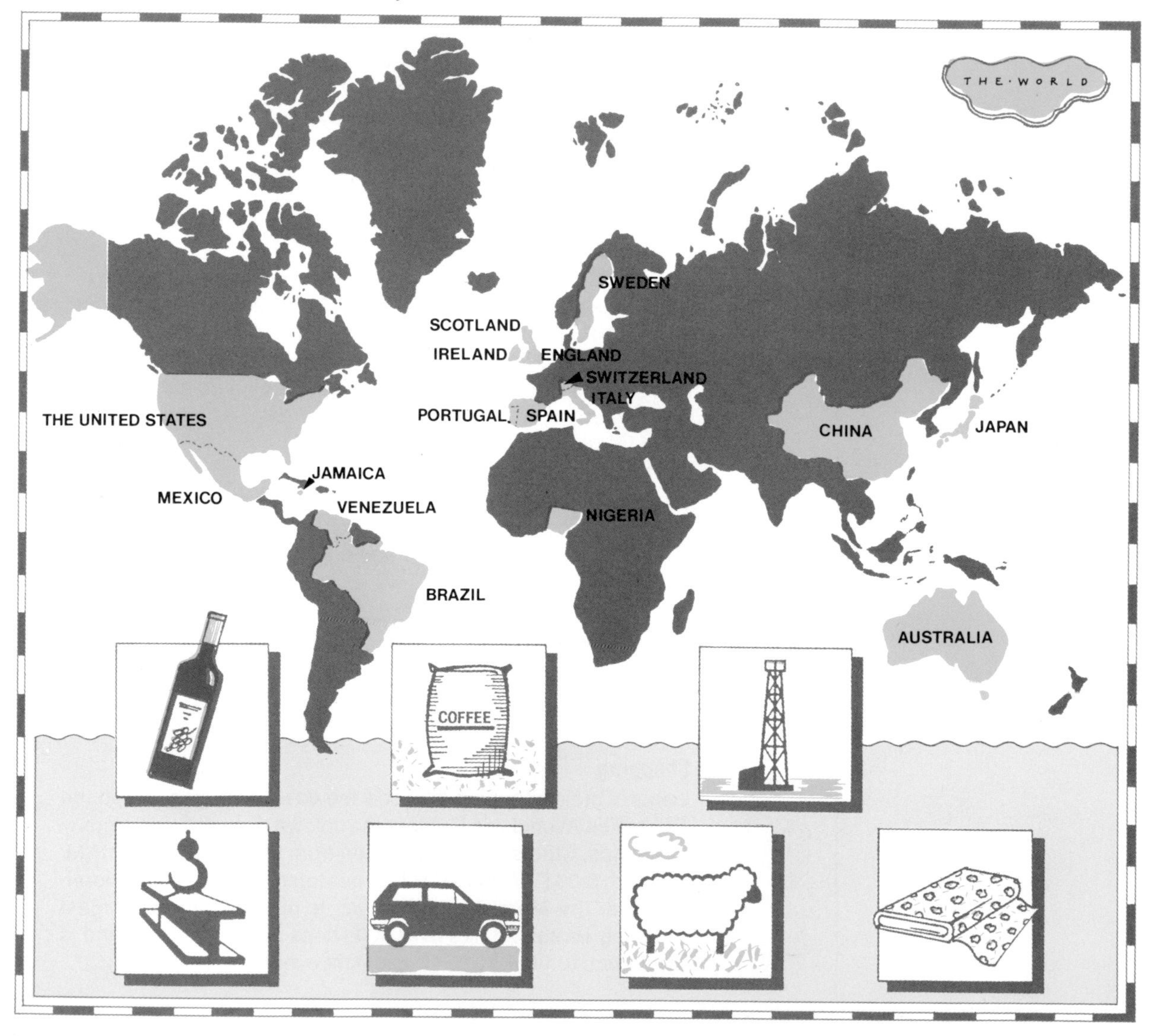

Use the words and phrases in the box to explain how you related the symbols to the countries. Use the example as a guide.

produces is famous for manufactures has a lot of grows

Spain produces a lot of wine.

B. Look at some more symbols:

Match these symbols with appropriate countries. Then use the words and phrases in the box to explain how you related the symbols to the countries.

has a lot of is famous for has a ________ climate is the capital of in ________ they speak ________.

A. Listen to these descriptions of three countries. Do you know what countries they are?

B. Each of the pictures below shows something about one of the three countries you have been learning about. Make a table like the one below on another sheet of paper. Then as you listen again, fill in the table with the name of each country and the numbers of the pictures that go with that country.

	Name	Pictures
Country 1		
Country 2		
Country 3		

C. Now use the pictures to form sentences about the countries.

A. Draw a map of your country on a separate piece of paper. Do you remember the symbols you used at the beginning of this unit? Draw the symbols on your map that apply to your country.

B. Exchange maps with one of your classmates and share facts about your two countries. If you are from the same country as your partner, talk about how your maps are similar or different.

INPUT

How much do you know about Canada? Working with your classmates, think of as many facts and impressions as you can about this country. Be sure to write them down on a list like the one below.

A. Listen to an interview with a Canadian girl. Does she mention any of the facts on your list?

B. Working with your classmates, try to remember some of the things the Canadian girl spoke about. Use the words and phrases below to help you:

Ontario
25 percent
bilingual

second largest
Toronto
Ottawa

25 million
hot
minus 20 degrees Celsius

LANGUAGE SUMMARY

Asking For and Giving Information About Countries

FUNCTIONS

- Giving information about countries:

They	grow wheat produce oil manufacture cars raise cattle speak Spanish	in	my country. Canada. Argentina. the United States. Mexico.

My country Spain Greece	has a tropical climate. belongs to the EEC. has a lot of tourists.

Greece Japan Italy	is famous for its beautiful scenery.

Washington, D.C. is the capital of the United States.
China is an agricultural country.
Sweden is located in northern Europe.
Portugal is a member of NATO.
Japan is an industrialized country.

- Asking for information about countries:

What kind of climate does Switzerland have?
What language do they speak in Australia?
What do they manufacture in Japan?
Where is Greece?
What's the population of Swaziland?
What's the capital of your country?
What is your country famous for?
Is Denmark a member of the EEC?
Is Ottawa the capital of Canada?

STRUCTURES

- Questions with *like* and answers:

What's the climate like in Portugal?
It's hot in summer, but it's rainy and cool in the winter.

What's the scenery like in Switzerland?
There are a lot of beautiful mountains and lakes.

What are the people like in Spain?
They're friendly and energetic.

What's the food like in India?
People eat a lot of rice, curries, and vegetables.

INTENSIVE PRACTICE

A

Match the cities and countries on the left with the words and phrases on the right. Then make statements.

1. Japan
2. Canada
3. Mexico City
4. Greece

a. four islands
b. a lot of tourists
c. Toronto
d. over 15 million

B

Use the cues to make affirmative and negative statements. Use the example as a guide.

(grow) cotton/wheat
They grow cotton, but they don't grow wheat.

1. (grow) rice/coffee
2. (manufacture) textiles/cars
3. (produce) oil/steel
4. (raise) sheep/cattle
5. (have) beautiful scenery/good beaches
6. (speak) French/German

C

There are lots of questions we can ask about geography. Working with a partner, ask questions using the information below as a guide.

1. population of the United States?
2. capital of your country?
3. climate in Mexico?
4. languages in Belgium?
5. produce in Japan?
6. largest river in South America?

D

Games

1. Divide into two teams. Your teacher will show each team the name of a familiar country. Then get ready. Your team has one minute to come up with as many facts as possible about the country. The team with the most correct facts wins.
2. Write down one fact about any country you wish. Your teacher will collect everyone's facts and use them to give the class a quiz. Be ready to defend your fact! The student with the best score on the quiz wins.

READING

A Look at the table of nouns, verbs, and adjectives below. Do you know what they mean? Change each of the words to another part of speech, depending on where you see the star.

Nouns	Verbs	Adjectives
★	destroy	
★	regulate	
production	★	
★	propose	
★		agricultural
development	★	
★	organize	
economy		★
decision	★	
★	unify	

B What do you know about the European Economic Community (the Common Market)? How many members are there? Read the text below to find out.

The European Common Market

Can countries with different customs, different languages, and different religions be friends? Can countries with a long history of war against each other learn to work together? The countries that belong to the European Common Market think they can.

At the end of 1945, Europe was destroyed by war. Some countries decided it was time for a change. In 1951, Holland, Belgium, Luxembourg, Italy, France, and West Germany signed the Treaty of Paris. This treaty formed the European Coal and Steel Community.

The union was a success, and in 1957, the six countries signed the Treaty of Rome. The countries that signed this document promised to work together for their economic and social development.

These countries are officially called the European Economic Community, but most people call them the Common Market. Other countries that joined the Common Market were Ireland, Denmark, Britain, Greece, Spain, and Portugal.

Many people hope that in the future the countries of Europe will belong to one democratic government. Some people think that it is a good way to put an end to war. The 12 countries that currently belong to the Common Market think it's a good beginning.

C

Complete the following statements about the Common Market. Work with a partner to try and think of several different ways to complete each one.

1. European countries have different . . . .
2. At the end of 1945, ...
3. In 1951, six countries . . . .
4. The Treaty of Rome . . . .
5. Maybe in the future there will be . . . .

WRITING

Interview a classmate who is from another city or country. You will need to ask a lot of questions. Make a form like the one below on another sheet of paper and use it to make notes. Then share your information with the rest of your classmates.

Name of Country/Region ______________________

Geography ______________________

Climate ______________________

Agriculture ______________________

Industry ______________________

People ______________________

4 I'm just looking, thank you.

PRESENTATION

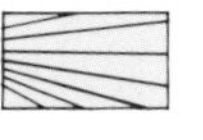

A. Cover up the bottom half of this page and then look at the pictures. What do you think the customers are saying? Discuss your ideas with your classmates.

1.

2.

3.

4.

5.

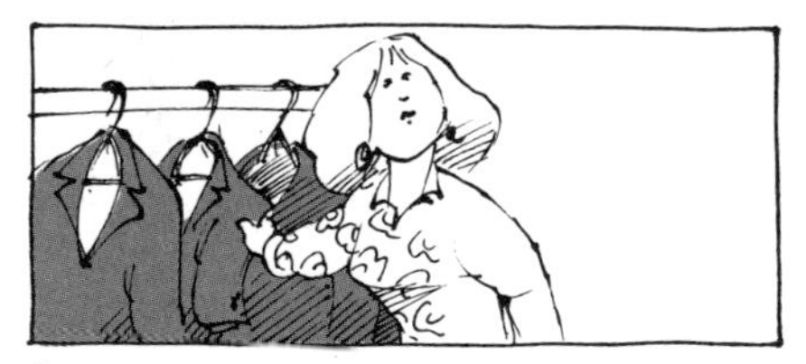

6.

a. Do you have this in a larger size?
b. Could I try this on?
c. I'll have the roast chicken, please.
d. I didn't want to spend that much.
e. Could I see that tennis racket, please?
f. I'll just have a glass of water.
g. It's too small.
h. Could you tell me the price of this blouse?
i. Do you have this in blue?
j. Do you have anything less expensive?
k. How much are those T-shirts over there?
l. I'm just looking, thank you.

B. Now uncover the list of comments and see if any of your ideas are there. Then match the comments to the pictures. Some of the comments can go with more than one picture.

A. Look at the shops and restaurants below. What are some things that are sold in each?

B. Listen to four conversations. In which shop or restaurant is each taking place?

C. Listen to the conversations again and write down, on a separate piece of paper, the words to fill in the numbered blanks.

1.

A: Hi. ___1___ help you?

B: ___2___ tell me the price of this squash racket, please?

A: ___3___ $65.50.

B: Hmmm. I didn't ___4___ that much. ___5___ are those jogging shorts?

A: $10.98.

B: Could I ___6___?

A: Sure. ___7___.

2.

A: How does it look?

B: ___1___ in a larger size, a 12, maybe?

A: I think so. Let me ___2___.

B: And ___3___ in dark blue?

A: Let me go and ___4___ for you.

3.

A: ___1___ help you, sir?

B: ___2___ looking for now, thanks.

A: Fine. If you ___3___ . . .

B: ___4___ that CD player, please?

A: Sure. We just got these in. They sound great—and there's a 15 percent ___5___, too.

B: Oh! ___6___ the compact discs, too?

A: No, you can ___7___ them at the record shop next door.

4.

A: Good evening. ___1___ ready to order?

B: Yes, ___2___ the lobster special, please.

A: What ___3___ to drink?

B: ___4___ some white wine, please. And could you ___5___ us an ashtray?

A: I'm afraid you're not in the ___6___. Would you like to move?

B: No, we'll ___7___.

Working with a partner, practice one of the dialogues that you have completed above. Then continue the dialogues on your own.

INPUT

Here are some things you can buy in any department store. What are the names of the items? How many other items can you and your classmates think of?

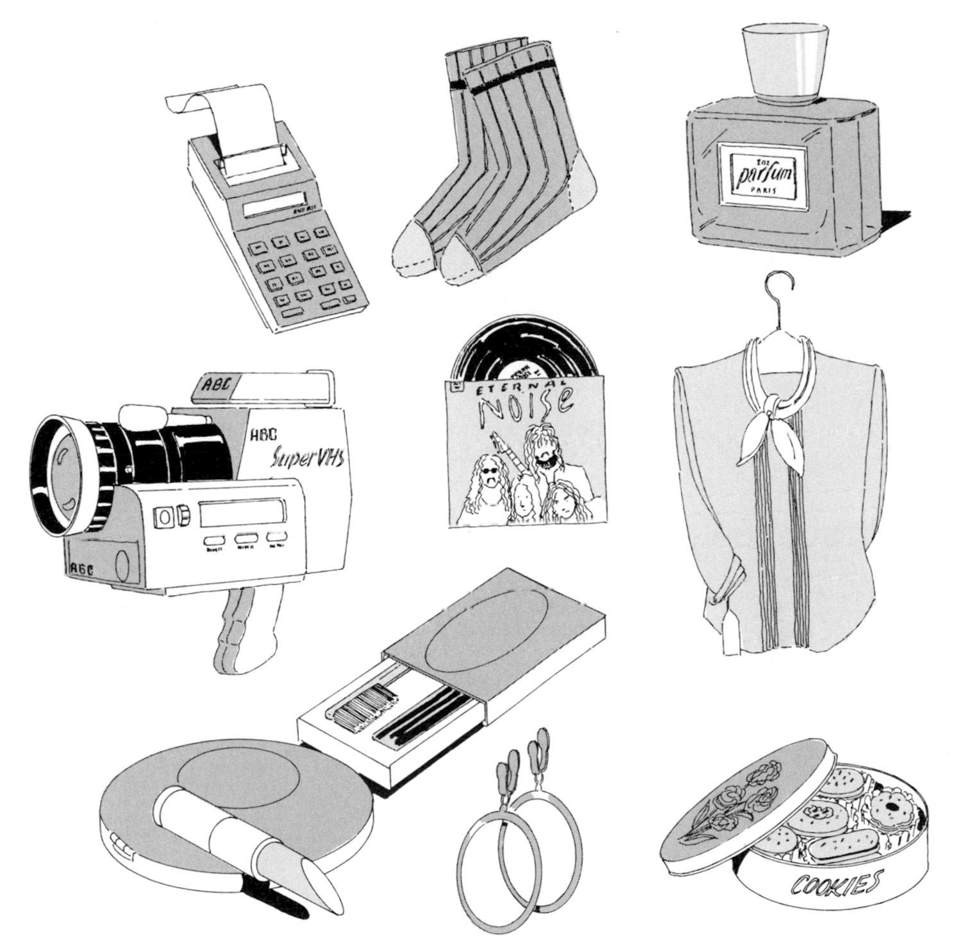

A. Paul is a 15-year-old boy. He is in a department store looking for a birthday present for his mother. List some of the problems Paul may have. For example, he may not know what colors his mother prefers.

B. Now listen to the conversation between Paul and a salesperson. What problems does Paul have? Did you guess any of them?

C. Look at the adjectives below. What do they mean? Listen to the conversation again. Which adjectives describe Paul and which ones describe Ms. Stacey? Compare your answers with those of your classmates.

confused polite kind selfish broke

LANGUAGE SUMMARY

Talking in Stores and Restaurants

FUNCTIONS

- Talking about prices in stores:

How much is this tennis racket?
I don't want to spend that much.
Do you have anything less expensive?

- Talking about items for sale:

Could I see that CD player, please?
Could I try on this jacket, please?
It's too small.

- Ordering food in a restaurant:

I'll have the beef Stroganoff, please.
I'll have a Super Burger with french fries, please.

- Asking for things in a restaurant:

Could you bring us an ashtray, please?
Could we have some more water, please?

STRUCTURES

- Polite requests with *could:*

Could you tell me the price of this coat, please?
Could I try it on?
Could I see that video camera, please?

- Use of *will* for ordering:

I'll just have a glass of water.
We'll have the lobster special.

- Questions with *have:*

Do you have it in a larger size?
Do you have it in blue?
Do you have anything less expensive?
Do you have any herb tea?
What do you have in size 12?
What kind of pie do you have today?

INTENSIVE PRACTICE

A

Practice asking the price of the items pictured below. For the first set of pictures, assume that you are holding the item and use *this* in your question. For the second set of pictures, assume that you are pointing to the item and use *that* in your question. Use the examples as guides.

Work with a partner and write a dialogue between a salesperson and a customer using the suggestions below.

SALESPERSON: Offer to help.
CUSTOMER: Reply that you are just looking. Then ask the price of a jacket you see.
SALESPERSON: Reply.
CUSTOMER: Ask for it in dark blue.
SALESPERSON: Show a dark blue jacket to the customer.
CUSTOMER: Ask to try it on.
SALESPERSON: Indicate the fitting room.
CUSTOMER: Thank the salesperson.

Complete the conversation in any way you wish.

Here is some useful restaurant language. Can you and your classmates think of any more items to add to the list?

Waiter
- Are you ready to order?
- What would you like to drink?

Customer
- Excuse me!
- I'll / We'll | have the roast chicken, please.

With a partner, practice ordering something to eat from the menu below. You should take turns being the waiter and the customer.

Chaplin's sandwich shop

MENU

SANDWICH SPECIALS

Hamburger	2.25
Cheeseburger	3.00
Grilled cheese sandwich	1.50
Chicken sandwich	1.95
Tunafish sandwich	1.75

SIDE ORDERS

French fries	1.00
Tossed salad	1.25

BEVERAGES

Milk	.75
Chocolate milk	.95
Coffee	.75
Tea	.75
Cola	.85
Milkshake	1.20

DESSERTS

Ice cream	1.00
Apple pie	1.70
Chocolate cake	1.65

READING

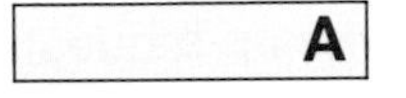

A

Every year men and women all over the world spend millions of dollars on health and beauty aids such as toothpaste, shampoo, soap, beauty creams, makeup, etc. These are products we use every day—but how much do we *think* about them before we buy them? Put your answers to this questionnaire on a separate sheet of paper to find out if you are a sensible shopper.

What's Your Health and Beauty Aid IQ?

	yes	sometimes	no
1. I try to buy natural products.	☐	☐	☐
2. It is better to buy products in spray cans than other types of packages.	☐	☐	☐
3. I am impressed by products that have scientific sounding ingredients — like X-E or T-49.	☐	☐	☐
4. The size of a package generally tells us how much of the product is inside.	☐	☐	☐
5. I like to buy health and beauty aids that smell nice.	☐	☐	☐
6. I forget to read the label before I buy a health or beauty aid.	☐	☐	☐
7. Practically all health and beauty aids made by big companies are safe to use.	☐	☐	☐

B

How did your classmates answer the questionnaire? Do their answers agree with yours? **Note**: If you answered *no* to most of the items in the questionnaire, you can consider yourself a sensible shopper!

WRITING

Here are some helpful suggestions for shoppers. Make up a questionnaire and see if your classmates are good shoppers or not. Half the class should write a questionnaire on the information in **A** and half the class should use the information in **B.** Then take turns giving your questionnaires to each other.

A	B
A good shopper always makes a list before going shopping. If you follow a list, you will not buy things that you don't really need. A sensible shopper is not influenced by advertising. It is better to talk to friends who can give you a personal opinion about the product. A good shopper also goes shopping when there aren't a lot of people in the stores. It is difficult to concentrate and make a decision if there are a lot of people around. A sensible shopper always looks at his receipt right after buying something.	A sensible shopper thinks twice before buying something. People often buy things they don't need and can't use. A good shopper always counts his change right after buying something. A sensible shopper never buys a product *only* because it's on sale. Stores often have sales to try and persuade people to buy things they don't need. A good shopper also supports local consumer organizations.

5 Do you remember when . . . ?

PRESENTATION

Look at the picture. Use the cues in the box to help you. Talk about events in your life with your classmates.

went to ________ (school)	met/got married
was/were born	moved/graduated from

A. You are going to listen to eight people talk about an important event in their lives. Number a sheet of paper from 1–8. Then, as you listen, put a plus sign (+) for each speaker who talks about a happy memory. Put a minus sign (−) for each speaker who talks about an unhappy memory.

B. Now listen again. As each person speaks, write down two or three words of what he or she says.

A. Look at the notes you took while listening. Then report to your classmates what one of the speakers said.

B. Do any of the events the people talked about remind you of something in your own life? Tell your classmates about your memory.

INPUT

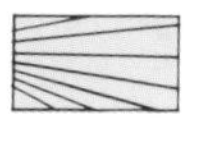

In 1986 the Nobel Prize for Literature was won by a Nigerian writer, Wole Soyinka. Look at the notes on his life below. What events do you think they refer to? Discuss your ideas with your classmates.

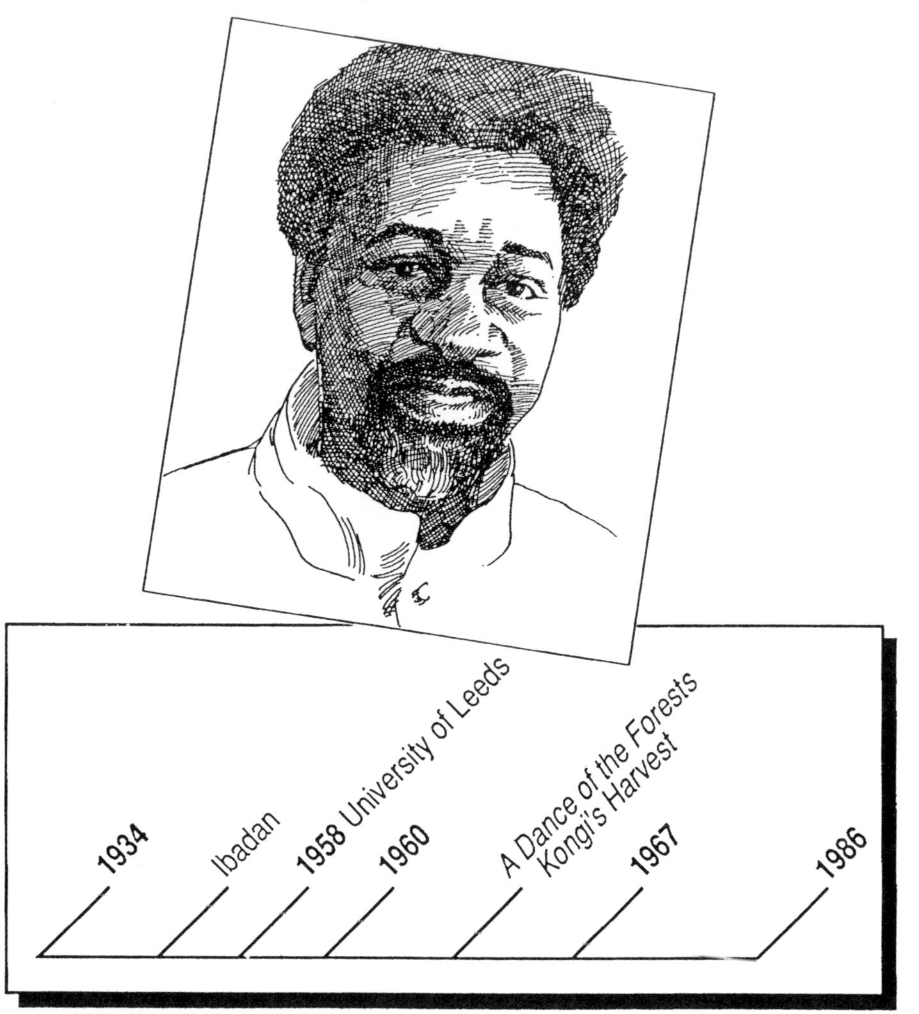

A. Now listen to a news broadcast about Soyinka and check to see if your ideas were correct.

B. Listen again. This time take notes on information about Wole Soyinka that is not referred to on Soyinka's timeline. Make a list with your classmates.

C. Think of a famous person in your country such as a writer, a singer, or an actor. Do you know any facts about the person's past? Tell your classmates what you know, and see whether they can guess who the person is.

LANGUAGE SUMMARY

Talking About Our Life History

FUNCTIONS

- Talking about our parents:

My parents met at a party.
They got married in 1968.

- Talking about our childhood:

I grew up in a small town.
We moved to New York when I was six years old.

- Talking about high school and college:

I went to North Carver High School.
I graduated from New York University.
I got my B.A. in English Literature.

- Talking about jobs:

I got a job after I graduated from college.
I worked as a radio announcer when I left school.

- Talking about other events:

I won a poetry prize in high school.
I met my wife when I was 25.

- Asking about someone's background:

Where were you born?
Did you move when you were young?
What high school/college did you go to?
What did you do after you left school?
When did you first meet your wife?

STRUCTURES

- Past tense statements and questions:

I went to public school in Oakville.
Where did you go to public school?
Did you go to public school in Oakville?

I worked as a copywriter for three years.
What did you do after college?
How long did you work as a copywriter?

- Statements and questions with *was/were:*

I was born in Ohio.
My father was born in Boston.
My brothers were born in Canada.
Were you born in Boston?
Were your brothers born in Canada?

Where were	you they	born?
Where was	he she	born?

INTENSIVE PRACTICE

Kevin Warren is an American writer who now lives in Japan. Working with a partner, use the information below to talk about his life.

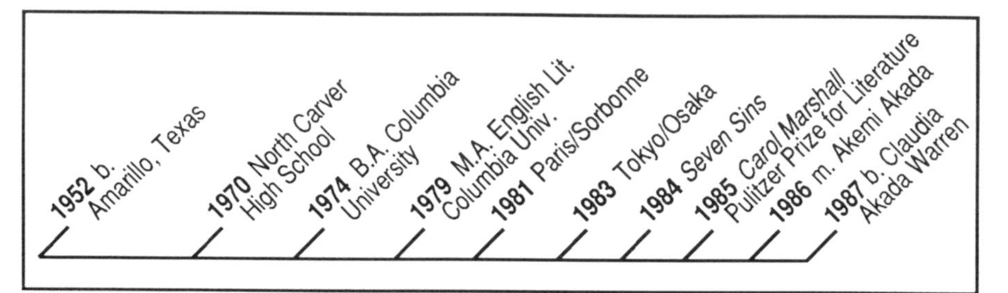

B

Look at the pictures below. Working with a group of your classmates, see if you can combine the pictures to tell an interesting story. Then compare your story with those of other groups.

Ask your classmates questions and try to find someone who—

1. was born on a holiday.
2. went to more than one high school.
3. moved when he or she was young.
4. learned to play a musical instrument.
5. played on a school team.

READING

A

Half of your class should read Part 1 and the other half Part 2. Afterwards, get together with someone who read a different part than you did and find out if the statements below your reading are true or false. Your partner should be able to give you the information you need and you should be able to supply the information your partner needs.

Michael J. Fox

Part 1

Michael J. Fox was born in Canada. He has four brothers and sisters. His father was in the Armed Forces, so Michael spent the first ten years of his life moving from one army base to another. Finally, his family decided to stay in British Columbia.

At 13 he learned to play the guitar and started performing with a rock band. He also first studied acting in high school. He was always a good student, but he decided to quit high school and move to Los Angeles to try a career in acting.

Michael was lucky in California. He appeared in several TV shows and in 1982 won the part of Alex P. Keaton in "Family Ties." The show became one of the most popular TV series in the United States and Michael became famous.

Find out from your partner if the following are true or false.

1. Michael J. Fox didn't think about careers when he was young.
2. He got a job acting on Canadian TV when he was a teenager.

continued

3. He has appeared in only one movie.
4. He looks older than he really is, so he usually plays mature men.

Michael J. Fox

Part 2

When Michael J. Fox was young, like many Canadian boys, he wanted to become a Mountie or a famous hockey player. But as he grew older he found something he liked better, so he changed his plans.

Michael always loved performing. When he was 15, he played a 10-year-old boy in a Canadian TV show. The show was a success, and Michael decided to become a professional actor.

While starring in a popular TV series, he received several movie offers and made *Back to the Future, Teen Wolf,* and *The Secret of My Success.* Although he is over 25, Michael usually plays teenage parts because he is short and looks so young.

Find out from your partner if the following are true or false.

1. Michael J. Fox is an only child.
2. His father is a businessman.
3. His family decided to live in British Columbia when he was a young boy.
4. Michael decided to quit school because he was a bad student.
5. In 1982 he got a part in the popular U.S. TV series "Family Ties."

WRITING

Read this pen-pal letter and write a similar one. Talk about your life, past and present, just like Anne Marie does.

Dear Carol,

Hi! Thanks for your letter. I was very interested in everything you told me about yourself. Now it's my turn, right?

Well, I work in the accounting department of a large bank here in Paris. I'm divorced and I have one child, a little girl.

A little personal history: I was born in Paris and went to primary school here, but then my parents moved to London and I went to high school there (I really learned a lot of English). A few years later we moved back to France (Paris again), where I went to the University. I graduated three years ago.

I like swimming, reading and going to the movies. I also enjoy meeting new people—so maybe some day we can visit each other.

Write soon,
Anne Marie

6 I get up at six o'clock every day.

PRESENTATION

These pictures show things that we do regularly as part of our daily routine. What verbs do we use to talk about these everyday activities?

A. Look at the people in the pictures below. Can you imagine what their daily routines are like? Write a possible daily routine for each person, choosing from the information in the box below. Then compare what you and your classmates have written.

> gets up at 6 or 8 A.M.
> has a large or small breakfast
> drives or walks to work
> gets to work at 8 or 9 A.M.
> eats lunch at work or at a restaurant
> leaves work at 5 or 9 P.M.
> works on the weekends or spends the weekends with the family

B. Now listen as Ellen and Kevin talk about their daily routines. Were your ideas about them correct?

Working with a partner, tell each other about your daily routines. Are your routines similar? Tell the class how your routine is similar to your partner's.

INPUT

Look at the people in the pictures. Then look at the words in the box. Try to decide with your classmates which word best describes each person.

A. Clara is talking to her friend Paula about a problem she has. Listen and see if you can find her problem in the list below.

1. She likes all her boyfriends and can't decide.
2. She is too critical.
3. She doesn't like any of her boyfriends.

B. Make a table like the one below on another sheet of paper. Then listen again. As Clara describes each boyfriend, write the adjective in the space next to his name that describes him best.

NAME	DESCRIPTION	FREE TIME ACTIVITIES
1. MIKE		
2. TONY		
3. DAVE		
4. JOHN		
5. JACK		
6. FRANK		

C. What does each of Clara's boyfriends do in his free time? Listen to the tape again and make notes in the right-hand column of your chart.

D. Now use your notes to talk about each of the people on the tape and their activities.

LANGUAGE SUMMARY

Talking About Daily Routines

FUNCTIONS

- Talking about daily activities:

I get up at 7:00 every day.
He usually drives to work.

- Asking about daily activities:

What time do you get up every day?
How does he get to work?

- Telling about weekend activities (free time/leisure):

I usually spend the weekend with my family.
He plays tennis on Saturdays.

- Asking about weekend activities:

What do you usually do on the weekend?
What does he do on Saturdays?

- Talking about frequency of regular activities:

I go to the movies about once a month.
He does his exercises every day.

- Asking about frequency of regular activities:

How often do you go to the movies?
How often does he do his exercises?

STRUCTURES

- Present tense:

I They	usually have breakfast at 8:00.
He She	usually has breakfast at 8:00.

What time do	you they	go shopping?
How often does	he she	go shopping?

INTENSIVE PRACTICE

The pictures below show different people doing a part of their daily routine. Look at each picture and think of as many questions as you can. Use the example as a guide.

What time does he get up every day?
Does he get up early every day?

1.

2.

3.

4.

Working with a partner, take turns asking and answering questions about the following pictures. Use the example as a guide.

twice a month

A: *How often do you go to the movies?*
B: *I go twice a month.*

1. every Saturday

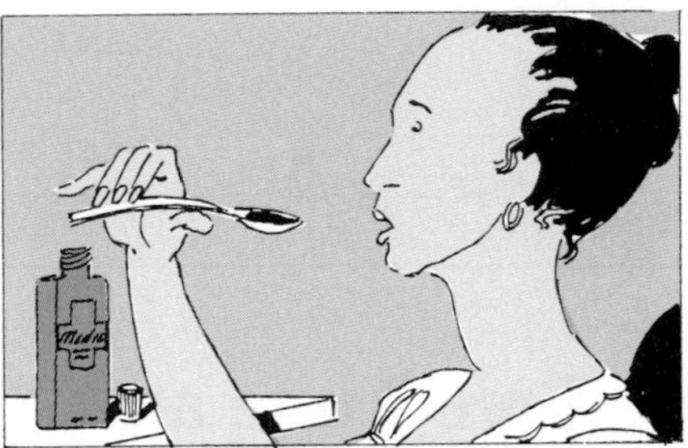

2. twice a day

3. twice a year

4. twice a week

5. every day

6. every weekend

C

Now ask the questions again. This time your partner will answer with real information about him or herself.

D

Ask your classmates questions and try to find someone who . . .

1. goes to the movies once a week.
2. goes to sports events once a month.
3. eats out twice a week.
4. goes shopping twice a week.
5. makes long-distance phone calls twice a month.
6. buys the newspaper every day.

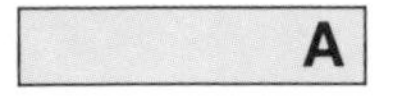

A

What is your favorite color? Do you believe that your favorite color reveals something about your personality? Read the text below.

Free Time and Your Favorite Color

Everybody has a favorite color. Some people prefer warm colors, like yellow and orange, while other people prefer cool colors, like blue and green. Some psychologists believe that a person's favorite color shows something about his or her personality. Below are descriptions of eight different personalities. As you read, decide which color fits your personality.

RED

If you like this color, you travel to faraway places on your vacations. You love parties with lots of music and dancing.

BLUE

If this is your favorite color, you love art and nature. In your free time you read history and art books—and also a few novels.

YELLOW

If you prefer this color, you like spending your time with other people. You go camping and fishing in your free time—usually with a group.

GREEN

People who like this color work very hard, because they feel they need more money. They don't have much free time.

GRAY

If you like this color, you are a sad person. You don't like parties or big groups of people. You probably watch TV on the weekend.

BROWN

If this is your favorite color, you like doing things around the house. You love family life and give a lot of parties at home.

ORANGE

If this is your favorite color, you enjoy meeting new people. During your vacation you like going to a lot of different places, because there are new people to meet everywhere.

PURPLE

Art is important to you if you prefer this color. You listen to music, paint, write, or go to the movies. You appreciate good food and drink.

B What is your partner's favorite color? Does the description for that color match his or her personality? Ask questions to find out. Use the example as a guide.

A: *What's your favorite color?*
B: *My favorite color is red.*
A: *Do you travel to faraway places on your vacations? Do you like parties with lots of music and dancing?*

WRITING

Read this letter from a college student to his parents. Then imagine that you are at one of the places listed below, and write a letter to your parents or a friend telling them what you do every day.

> *Dear Mom and Dad,*
>
> *So far I'm having a difficult time here. I get up at 7:00 A.M. because my first class is at eight. Sometimes I get up late, so I only have a cup of coffee for breakfast. I have five classes a day, and I only get back to my room around 5:00 P.M. I usually study until midnight.*
>
> *I miss your cooking, Mom. I eat at the cafeteria twice a day, but the food is terrible. Could you please send me some money? I need about . . .*

1. your grandparents' farm
2. an army training camp
3. a luxury hotel
4. a health spa
5. a campground

7 Nice to meet you, too.

PRESENTATION

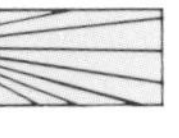

The conversations for the two situations pictured below are not in the correct order. Working in small groups, put the sentences in order so that the conversations make sense. There may be more than one order.

Sylvia is introducing Mei Ling, an exchange student, to her friend, Phil.

Barbara and Kevin haven't seen each other for a long time.

—Nice to meet you, Mei Ling.
—How long have you been here?
—Bye Mei Ling. Bye Phil. Take care.
—No, I'm from Boston but I've been here ten years.
—Phil, this is Mei Ling. She's from Hong Kong.
—About three months. Are you from New York?
—Nice to meet you, too.

—We're all fine. Janet's working now, part time.
—Barbara? What a surprise! What are you doing here?
—I sure will. Take care of yourself, now. It was great seeing you!
—That's great! Give her my love, will you?
—Kevin Wilson! I don't believe it!
—I'm visiting my brother for a few days. And how have you been? How's Janet?

Sylvia is having a party. Some of the people she has invited do not know each other. Look at the picture below as you listen to four conversations. Which people know each other? Which people are meeting for the first time?

Working with a partner, pretend that you are meeting one another for the first time at a party. Ask and answer questions about each other. Use ideas from the previous dialogues to help you.

INPUT

Have you ever been embarrassed because you forgot someone's name? What's the best thing to do in this situation? Compare your ideas with those of your classmates.

A. Listen to what happens when George doesn't recognize a person he has met before.

B. The people in the conversation talked about their children. Make a form like the one below on another sheet of paper. Then listen to the conversation again and write down what each of their children is doing.

Mike	
Marli	
Marion	
Kathy	

LANGUAGE SUMMARY

Talking With People We Meet

FUNCTIONS

- Introducing someone:

Phil, this is Mei Ling.
David, have you met Caroline?

- Meeting someone for the first time:

Nice to meet you, Mei Ling.
Nice to meet you, too.

- Meeting an old friend:

Expressing surprise:
I don't believe it. What are you doing here?
What a surprise!

Greetings:
How've you been?
Just fine. How about you?
It's so good to see you.

Commenting on appearance:
You look great.
You look as beautiful as ever.

Asking about other people:

How's Mary?	What's Mike doing these days?
She's fine.	He's living in New York now.

Saying good-bye:
Take care (of yourself).
It's been great seeing you.
Say hi to Susan for me.
Give Mary my love.

STRUCTURES

- Present progressive tense:

What's	Bob Marli	doing?

He's She's	studying at NYU.

Is	he she	still working at the bank?

- Present perfect tense:

How long have you been there?

How long has	he she	been there?

I've He's She's	worked there for six months.

INTENSIVE PRACTICE

Ask a question beginning with "how long" for each of the statements below. Use the example as a guide.

The Smiths are in California now.
How long have they been there?

1. Mr. Campbell is at IBM now.
2. They're divorced now.
3. My father's retired now.
4. Betty is a doctor now.
5. My brother's married now.
6. Colleen's parents are separated.
7. Laura's at the University of Michigan now.
8. I'm working at the phone company now.

Ask and answer questions using the words and pictures below as a guide.

your brother/Nova University?

Is your brother still going to Nova University?
No, he's working in an office now.

1. your parents/Ohio?

2. your boyfriend/in a band?

3. your mother/high school?

4. you/that small apartment?

5. you/exercise classes?

6. your husband/the personnel department?

C

Make a card like the one below on another sheet of paper. Use the names of three people you are close to, either family members or friends.

NAMES OF FAMILY OR FRIENDS
1. ________ 3. ________
2. ________

Now find a partner and exchange cards. Greet each other and then ask each other about the people on one another's cards. Use the example as a guide.

A: Hi, ________ , how are you?
B: Great! How about you?

A: Oh, I'm fine. How's________? What's she doing these days?
B: She's fine. She's still working at the same place . . . And how's ________?

READING

A

Do you have a good memory? Here's a way to test it. Look carefully at picture 1 for 45 seconds. Then turn the page to look at picture 2. There are 6 differences. List as many as you can. Then compare your list with those of your classmates.

B You are going to read an article about memory. But first scan the article and make a list of any words you don't know. Then read the article.

Title:

When you ask people if they have good memories, they usually say no. In fact, most people think that their memories are terrible. "I can never remember a new person's name," they say, or "I can remember the facts for an exam, but then I forget almost everything right away."

But psychologists say that it is normal to forget. "Many people think that all information stays in the brain forever," says one psychologist. "But much information only stays in the brain for 30 seconds, and then we lose it."

There are some things you can do to improve your memory. One memory specialist suggests that repetition is important. When we repeat something, we remember it better. When you are introduced to a person, repeat his or her name: "Nice to meet you, Bob." "How are you, Mary?" Then use the person's name several times during the conversation: "Where are you from, Barbara?" "So, Mike, where do you work?"

A second suggestion is to associate a person's name with an image or picture in your mind. When you meet the person again, you may remember the image. For example, if the person's name is Alexander Rivers, you can think of Alexander the Great standing near a large river.

A third suggestion is to make a list of the new people you meet. Then look at the list occasionally to refresh your memory.

Psychologists say that having a good memory is like being a good student. You have to work at it.

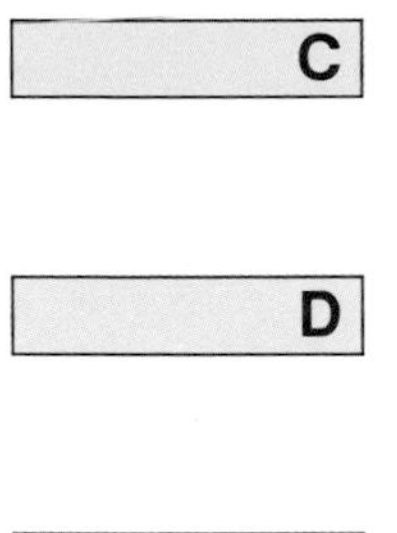

C The article does not have a title. Think about the content of the article (or read it again) and choose an appropriate title. Compare your title with those of your classmates. Do you agree with everybody's title?

D Look at the list of words you made before you read the article. Do you know the meanings now? If not, use a dictionary to help you share the definitions with your classmates.

E Working with a partner, create two true/false questions about the article to ask your classmates.

WRITING

A Can you change these sentences so that the words are in the proper order? Write your answers on a sheet of paper.

1. advertising is for Bill now company an working.
2. usual I'm hard as working.
3. Hi! you How've been?
4. computer still Is courses taking he?
5. family is your How in everyone?
6. been months there He's six for.
7. all We're fine.
8. Phillip is How?
9. you bank the Are working still at?
10. also courses the taking two university at I'm.

B Use the sentences in exercise A to complete the following letter on another sheet of paper. You will have to put the sentences in a logical order.

Dear Cathy,

____________________?

____

____

____

____

____

____________________?

____________________?

____________________?

____________________?

Write soon and tell me all the news!

Love,

Felicity

8 So, what did you do?

PRESENTATION

Look at the pictures and choose one that shows something that you did recently. Tell your classmates about it. Use the words in the box to help you.

last	night week month	yesterday on the weekend during my vacation	a few	days weeks	ago

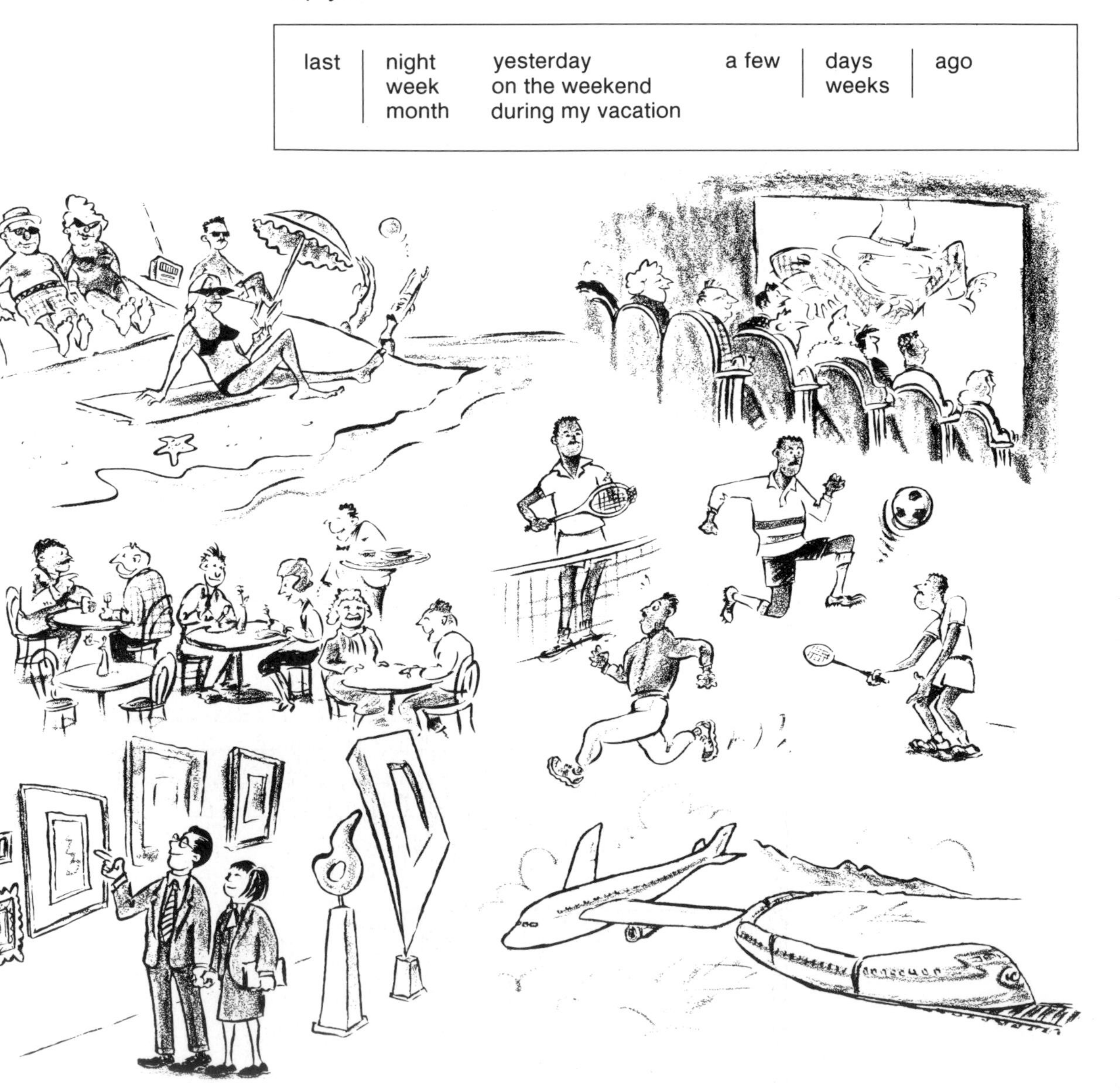

A. You are going to hear three people talk about things they did recently. As you listen to each conversation, write down the numbers of the pictures that show something that is being talked about.

Conversation 1

Conversation 3

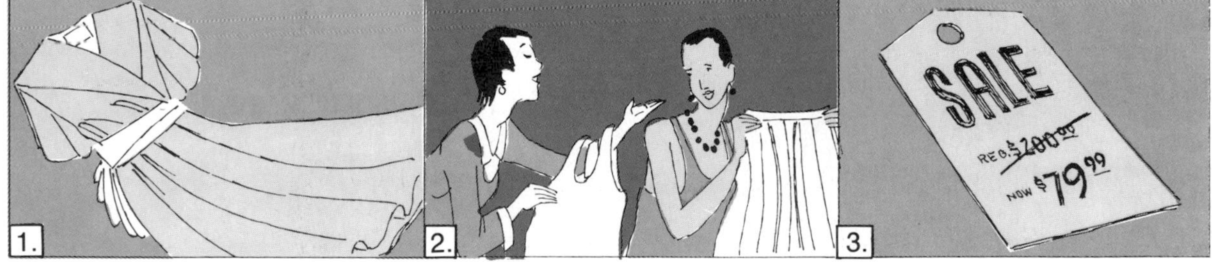

B. Look at the pictures again. Use the information in the conversations to talk about each one.

With your classmates, make a list of activities you do on weekends. You can use the verbs in the box below and any other verbs you think of. Then work with a partner to ask and answer questions about each other's weekends. Whenever you get a "yes" answer, ask for more information.

Did you go to the movies Saturday night?

go	sleep (late)	watch	buy	eat	play

INPUT

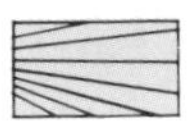

Think of the last time you . . . .

Tell your classmates about it.

A. Listen to a young man named Mark talk about his day. What did he do?

B. What Mark said about his day is mysterious because he doesn't tell us the details of what he did. For example: *Who did he meet downtown? What kind of newspaper ad was it?* As you listen again, make notes on the facts Mark left out.

C. Use your notes to think of questions about Mark's day. Make a list of at least three questions. Then, working with a partner, think of some possible answers to your questions. For example: *Maybe he met his girlfriend downtown. It was an ad about a car for sale.*

D. Now listen to Mark tell us about his day again—this time with all the details. Were any of your answers right?

LANGUAGE SUMMARY

Talking About Recent Activities

FUNCTIONS

- Talking about recent activities:

So what did you do	last night?
	last week?
	yesterday?

I went to the movies.
We went to the beach.
I played tennis.

- Talking about vacations:

How was your vacation?
It was great.
We went to Paris.
We stayed in a very nice hotel.
We bought lots of souvenirs.

STRUCTURES

- Past tense:

What did you do on the weekend?
I went downtown.
We went out to dinner.
Where did you go on your vacation?
I went to Rio.
We visited relatives in Hong Kong.
Where did you buy your new coat?
I bought it at Macy's.

INTENSIVE PRACTICE

Working with a partner, create a short dialogue for each of the following pictures. Imagine that the action took place in the recent past. Use the example as a guide.

A: *Where did you go on your vacation?*
B: *I went to Amsterdam.*
A: *Really? What airline did you go on?*
B: *KLM.*
A: *Did you go alone?*
B: *No, I went with my brother.*

1.

2.

3.

4.

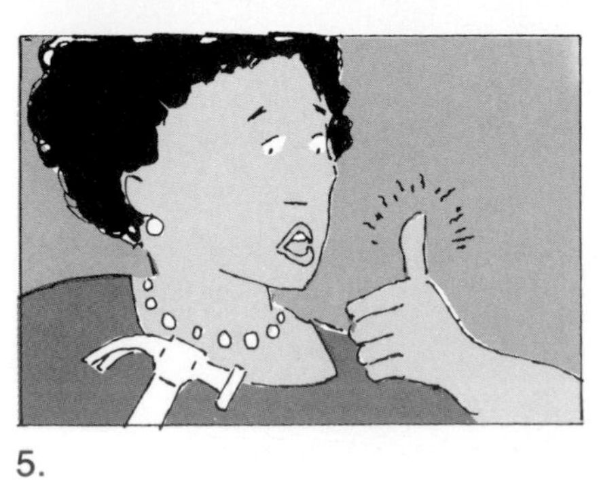

5.

6.

B

Divide into two teams. Group A, think of something you did recently and write a sentence about it on a small piece of paper. For example: *I made a long-distance phone call yesterday.* Put your sentence into a box along with those of your classmates. Group B, mix up the sentences in the box and pass it around so that everyone can pick a sentence. Now get up and find the person who wrote the sentence you picked. You will need to ask your classmates "Did you . . . " questions until you find a person who says "yes." For example:

Did you make a long-distance phone call yesterday?

Then sit down with the person and ask as many questions as you can think of. For example:

Who did you call?
Why did you phone him (or her)?
What country did you call?

Now reverse your jobs. Group B, you will write the sentences. Group A, you will mix them up and choose from Group B's sentences.

C

Make sentences using the cues below. Use the example as a guide.

(pay) telephone bill/water bill
I paid the telephone bill, but I didn't pay the water bill.

1. (go) the movies/the theater
2. (buy) a TV/a computer
3. (see) John/Mary
4. (read) the newspaper/the magazine
5. (have) lunch/dessert

D

Look at Janet's datebook. Do you know what all the abbreviations mean? If not, ask your classmates. Janet put a check (✓) beside the things that she did. The things that she *didn't* do are *not* checked. Talk with your classmates about the things Janet did each day.

MON.	appt: w/Dr. Evans — 10 A.M. ✓ lunch w/Judy	THURS.	shirt for dad — XL
TUES.	get package from P.O. ✓ Xmas presents ✓	FRI.	Mom & Dad arr. TWA flt. 206 9:00 A.M. ✓ party — Joe & Linda's
WED.	hairdresser appt. — 12:30 ✓ car to Anderson's Garage	SAT.	Macbeth Perf. Arts Ctr. 9:30 ✓
		SUN.	

READING

Towns and villages often have small newspapers that report local news and interesting facts about local people.
Read the "People" section of the *Camden-Exeter News* or the *Josdale Gazette.* Then get together with a partner who read a different newspaper than you did and ask him or her questions. Use the suggestions below each text for your questions.

Camden-Exeter News

Melissa Jones and Harry Carson were married in Exeter Church yesterday. Melissa, a sound engineer, works for CDC Records. Harry is a math teacher at Exeter High. The couple will be honeymooning in Jamaica.

Theodore Hughes of Camden opened his new vegetarian restaurant yesterday. The restaurant is on Baldwin Avenue and is Exeter's first vegetarian restaurant. We wish Theodore success in his new business!

The Dressers of Camden finally returned from their long vacation to the Far East. During their trip, which lasted six months, they visited Thailand, China, Hong Kong, Singapore, and Japan. Mr. Dresser, who retired last May, said that the trip was very memorable. Welcome back!

Now ask your partner about:
—Josdale's new doctor and why she decided to come to Josdale.
—a big party that was held in the Josdale Town Hall.
—Doug Vega and what happened to make him very happy.

The Josdale Gazette

Josdale welcomes its new doctor—Marilyn Kale, M.D. Dr. Kale arrived at the beginning of the month and officially started her practice on the 15th. Before coming to Josdale, she practiced at County Hospital in Albany, New York, for a year. She wanted to come to a small town "because it's more peaceful and the people are friendlier than in the city."

More than 250 people attended the retirement party held in the Josdale Town Hall last Saturday for Bonnie and Murray Bishop. The Bishops, former owners of the Good-Buy Supermarket, sold their business last month to a large supermarket chain.

Doug Vega, our local painter and sculptor, was very pleased with the interest shown in his first local exhibit. He sold 15 paintings and 2 sculptures to art lovers not only from Josdale but from Camden and Exeter as well.

Now ask your partner:
—what happened at Exeter church yesterday.
—about the Dressers, a local couple who took a long vacation.
—about Theodore Hughes and the new business he opened.

WRITING

A

Make a datebook page like the one below on another sheet of paper. Then try to remember the things that you did this week and enter them in the datebook. If you wish, you can use abbreviations like Janet did in her datebook on page 61.

MON.
TUES.
WED.
THURS.
FRI.
SAT.
SUN.

B

The English language uses capital letters in a lot of different situations. Here are some cases where capitals are used:

- names of people
- names of places
- names of rivers, mountains, etc.
- the first word in a sentence
- names of institutions
- holidays
- languages
- nationalities
- days of the week
- months
- family relationships before names (Cousin Joe)

Below is a page from Joe's journal. Copy what Joe has written on another sheet of paper, putting in capital letters where they are needed.

Tuesday, Feb. 4

today after french class barbara and i had lunch at mario's. it's a great place to eat and has the best italian food in town. i met a guy there from sicily who works with uncle joe. he arrived in the U.S. a year ago, and his english is already pretty good. his son goes to georgetown university.

after lunch we went for a walk along the trenton river. next wednesday we're going to a concert in camden park to hear the works of a brazilian composer— villa lobos. barbara says he's great! she heard some of his music last christmas in new york.

9 Tell me about your plans.

PRESENTATION

What plans did you have for your life when you were younger? What did you want to do or be? Share your thoughts with your classmates.

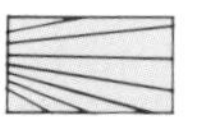

A. Listen to three people talk about their plans. They are all very sure of the future—too sure, maybe? As you listen, take notes on what they plan to do.

B. Now look at pictures of the people you have been listening to—Kim, Charles, and Dave. As you listen to them again, concentrate on the information that is listed under their pictures.

Kim	Charles	Dave
actress	school	uncle
Hollywood	father's company	motorcycles
MGM	vice president	California
Beverly Hills	married	gold

A. Now you've heard Kim, Charles, and Dave talk about their plans. What do you think is going to happen to them? Choose one person and decide what you think is going to happen to him or her. Then trace his or her life on the "map" on the next page.

B. Compare your life maps with those of your classmates. Use "going to" when explaining the route you chose.

INPUT

The five people below are all planning to help others in their countries. Look at the pictures beside them. What do you think they are planning to do? Discuss your ideas with your classmates.

A. Listen to the five people talk about their plans and see if your ideas were correct.

B. Make a table like the one below on another sheet of paper. Then listen to the five people again. As they talk, decide which of their plans are definite, which are dreams, and which are just possibilities. Then list their plans in the appropriate spaces in the table.

	DEFINITE PLANS	DREAMS	POSSIBILITIES
Daniel			
Ken			
Tina			
Mario			
Jayah			

C. Interview one of your classmates and find out what his or her plans are for the future. Then report what you find out to the class.

LANGUAGE SUMMARY

Talking About Future Plans

FUNCTIONS

- Talking about definite future plans:

I'm going to buy a new car next month.
They're planning to get married in April.

- Talking about indefinite wishes and plans:

I'd like to get my master's degree some day.
We're hoping to move to New York someday.

- Talking about possibilities:

I might open my own business, or I might work for my uncle. I'm not sure yet.

STRUCTURES

- Future with *going to:*

He's going to start a children's clinic in his village.

- Future with *planning to/hoping to:*

They're planning to go to Spain on their vacation.
I'm hoping to find a better job some day.

- Possibilities with *might:*

They might come to visit us, but they aren't sure yet.

INTENSIVE PRACTICE

Look at each of the pictures below and tell what you think is going to happen. Use the example as a guide.

The book is going to fall on his head.

1.

2.

3.

4.

5.

6.

B

Use the groups of words below and *might* to make sentences. Use the example as a guide.

my mother/visit/us
My mother might come to visit us, but she's not sure yet.

1. we/buy/a new car
2. my parents/go/Spain
3. I/start/a business
4. Darla/go/drama school
5. I/go away/this weekend
6. Jason/work for/his father
7. I/go/movies tonight

Use the words in parentheses to complete the following sentences. Use the example as a guide.

Jack is studying medicine because . . . (plan/doctor)
Jack is studying medicine because he's planning to become a doctor.

1. We're saving our money because . . . (hope/a new house)
2. When I graduate from college . . . (I'd like/Paris)
3. Before my brother goes to Italy . . . (plan/Italian lessons)
4. If I can borrow enough money . . . (hope/my own business)
5. When I finish school . . . (plan/handicapped children)
6. Some day, when I have more time . . . (I'd like/aerobics classes)

D

Choose one of the topics below and talk to your classmates about your plans. Tell them whether you have definite plans or whether your plans are possibilities or just dreams.

a new house
a master's degree
a trip somewhere
a business
a lot of money

a different job
a new car
helping people
working with children
other

READING

A

You are going to read a text in which the following words appear:

natural resources—products made by nature
environment—surroundings
national parks—areas of historical, scientific or scenic interest for use and enjoyment by the public
wildlife—animals living freely in a natural environment
electric power—a form of energy
dam—a barrier built across a river or lake to hold back water
valley farmland—a long low area between hills
fuel—material burned as a source of warmth, light or energy

Try to use each one of these words and phrases in a sentence. Here are ten verbs that you may find helpful.

develop	preserve	control	build
promote	destroy	create	provide
take care of	replant		

B

Read the text below. As you read, notice how the words from Part A are used in the text.

Planning for the Future

The world is beginning to understand the importance of conservation. If we want our planet to survive, we will have to take care of our natural resources. But can we develop economically and preserve the environment at the same time? Experts believe that development and conservation should go hand in hand.

Tamarin (not its real name) is an example of a developing country that is planning to manage its natural resources and preserve its environment. At the same time, the government is hoping to promote the country's *economic* development.

Last year, the National Planning Commission of Tamarin made some important decisions:

- **To create more national parks for the protection of Tamarin wildlife.**
- **To bring electric power to villages and rural areas by building dams; not to build these dams in areas where rich valley farmland will be destroyed.**
- **To manage forests that exist now and to replant forests that were cut down. This will control erosion and provide fuel for many villages.**

Like many countries, Tamarin is investing in its future before it is too late.

Answer these questions based on the reading.

1. How is Tamarin going to preserve the environment? How is Tamarin planning to promote economic development?
2. What is Tamarin *going to do* about each of the following?
   a. economic development
   b. national parks
   c. electric power
   d. dams
   e. forests
   f. replanting

WRITING

Nick and Marion are planning their summer vacation. After discussing the possibilities, Marion wrote some notes about their plans. Look at Marion's notes below. Can you tell what they are planning to do? What plans seem definite? What plans are just possibilities? Write down all the information you can from the notes.

Notes on trip:
Nick's vacation this year — July 15th - August 10th ✓ (confirmed)
London? — no — big city, too crowded X
Paris?? — expensive; too many tourists X
Spain! — Costa del Sol Benidorm/Torremolinos
Iberia or TWA New York/Madrid
then — rent a car — 2 or 3 weeks (depending on $)

things to buy: me — pottery, souvenirs, leather shoes
Nick — leather jacket??

things to do (if possible):
— bus tour to Seville and Cordoba
— flamenco!
— persuade Nick to go to Morocco — 2 days

10 Let's make some comparisons.

PRESENTATION

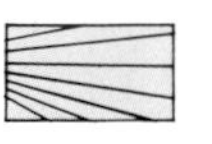

English, like other languages, has special rules for making comparisons. Can you and your classmates discover from the samples below what some of these rules are? (Hint: Notice the number of syllables in the adjectives.)

old	intelligent	prettier than
expensive	funny	taller than
pretty	older than	more intelligent than
tall	more expensive than	funnier than

Choose the pair of pictures that go with each conversation. Listen for the words that describe the pairs. Make a list of the adjectives that go with each.

Working with a partner, choose a pair of items pictured above and write a comparison dialogue using A and B instead of the names of the items. Then perform your dialogue for the class and see whether your classmates can guess which items you are talking about.

INPUT

A. Here are pictures of two sisters, Kathy and Julie, when they were younger. How do they seem to be different? Discuss your ideas.

B. Form a line with your classmates. The person with the most brothers and sisters goes to the end of the line. The person with the fewest (or no) brothers and sisters goes to the front. You will have to ask each other questions and organize the line yourselves.

C. Now sit down with one of the people standing next to you in line. Tell him or her about *one* of your brothers or sisters and how you are the same or different. Then listen while your partner tells about a brother or sister. If you don't have a brother or sister, talk about another family member or friend.

A. Listen to Kathy talk about her sister Julie. Can you tell *where* she is? Does she mention any of the things you noticed when you compared her picture with Julie's?

B. Listen again and write down the descriptive words and phrases that Kathy uses when she talks about her sister.

C. Now use the words you wrote down to talk with your classmates about the two sisters.

LANGUAGE SUMMARY

Making Comparisons

FUNCTIONS

- Comparing people:

People from the country are usually friendlier than people from the city.
She's older than her sister.
Charlie is doing better in school this term.
I get up earlier than Luis does.

- Comparing things:

Motorcycles are more dangerous than cars.
Your clothes will be cleaner with Whiz.
The movie was worse than we expected.

- Comparing according to size:

Which country is larger, Canada or the USSR?
Lake Superior is larger than Lake Victoria.
The anaconda snake of South America is 30 feet long—much longer than the king cobra of India.

STRUCTURES

- Rules for forming the comparative:

1. With one-syllable adjectives, add *-er:*
   longer than smaller than faster than
2. With adjectives of more than two syllables, use *more:*
   more flexible than more intelligent than
3. With two-syllable adjectives ending in *-y,* change the *y* to *i* and add *-er:*
   healthier than friendlier than dirtier than
4. With two-syllable adjectives that do not end in *-y,* use *more:*
   more active than more thorough than more helpful than
5. Sometimes the comparative is expressed with *less . . . than:*
   less tired than less comfortable than
   But usually *not as . . . as* is used:
   not as tired as not as comfortable as
6. *Good* and *bad* have irregular comparatives:
   good → better than bad → worse than

INTENSIVE PRACTICE

Work with a partner. Use the cues below to ask and answer questions. Use the example as a guide.

(large) Lake Superior/Lake Victoria
A: *Which lake is larger, Lake Superior or Lake Victoria?*
B: *I think Lake Superior is larger.*

1. (long) Nile River/Amazon River
2. (small) Monaco/Liechtenstein
3. (heavy) an American Greyhound bus/an English double-decker bus
4. (high) Mount McKinley/Kilimanjaro
5. (long) blue whale/elephant
6. (big) Madagascar/Great Britain
7. (fast) cheetah/ostrich
8. (tall) the World Trade Center in New York/the Sears Tower in Chicago
9. (more calories) ten ounces of boiled rice/ten ounces of boiled potatoes
10. (close to the Earth) Venus/Mars

B

Use the comparative of the word in parentheses to complete each of the following sentences. Use the example as a guide.

(early) Jack gets up ________ than I do.
Jack gets up earlier than I do.

1. (clean) London is ________ than it was ten years ago.
2. (humid) The winters in Europe are generally ________ than in the U.S.
3. (happy) Bill and Joan are ________ since they moved to Boston.
4. (bad) The concert was ________ than we expected.
5. (luxurious) Have you ever seen a ________ car?
6. (crowded) The subway is ________ than it was yesterday.
7. (interesting) Our English class was ________ than usual today.
8. (tall) Philip is ________ than his brother.
9. (friendly) Country people are often ________ than city people.
10. (good) The book was ________ than the film.

Advertising slogans often use comparatives. Working with a partner or a small group, write slogans that use comparatives for each of the products pictured below. Use the example as a guide.

Fresher, cleaner clothes with Whiz.

1.

2.

3.

4.

5.

6.

D

Talk with a partner about your daily routines and your families. Make a note of any differences you discover. Then tell your classmates about how you and your partner are different. For example:

I get up earlier than Marta. I have a bigger family. I eat a smaller breakfast than she does. My brother is older than hers.

A

There are many interesting stories about twins and how they are the same. Do you know any twins? How are their lives and personalities the same or different? Read the text below to find out more about twins.

Different But the Same

When twins Jim and Alex were born on October 14, 1947, their mother gave them up for adoption. Jim was adopted by the Wilsons. They lived in a small house in the country. Alex was adopted by the Perestrellos. They lived in a bigger house in the suburbs of a city. The Wilsons were a big family. They attended church regularly and were well-liked in their community. The Perestrellos were wealthier and more educated. Alex Perestrello went to private schools and had more opportunities as he was growing up than his brother, Jim Wilson.

When they were 35, the two brothers were part of a study. Scientists were examining the behavior of twins. The scientists discovered that Alex was not richer, more ambitious, more successful, or more educated than his brother. The brothers were more similar than different. They were both engineers, were both married to women named Barbara and both had two children. And they both drove white Chevrolets. They even had dogs with the same name—Bowser.

Scientists who study twins separated at birth have found that environment helps to form your personality, but your genes seem to be more important than the place you grew up or the people you lived with as a child.

B

Can you answer these questions?

1. What were the differences between Alex's family and Jim's family?
2. In what ways were the brothers the same as adults?
3. What did the scientists find out?

WRITING

Below is Charlie's report card for the first semester. As you can see, he was not a very good student.

COLUMBUS ELEMENTARY SCHOOL

Student Report
Semester 1 - Grade 5

A - Excellent **B - Very Good** **C - Average** **D - Below Average** **F - Failure**

Subject	Grade	Comments
History	D	Charlie is not trying hard enough.
English	F	Charles is lazy, reads slowly, has sloppy handwriting.
Social Studies	D	Charles doesn't pay attention in class.
Physical Education	C	Charles doesn't participate in group games.
Math	F	Charles doesn't concentrate, does careless work.
Behavior	U	Unsatisfactory — Charles is often noisy and disobedient in class.
Personal Habits	U	Unsatisfactory— Charles is not organized.

During the second semester Charlie has been doing much better. His teacher has been very pleased with his work. Here are the grades she plans to give him.

History—B
English—B−
Social Studies—A
Math—C+
Physical Education—B+
Behavior—good
Personal Habits—satisfactory

Draw a form like the report card above on another sheet of paper. Then, working with a partner, fill in the grades Charlie is to receive. Also, try to imagine what comments the teacher might make and write them in. Your comments should explain why Charlie's grades are so much better this term than they were last term.

Tapescript

Chapter 1, Page 1, Presentation

INTERVIEW 1

Interviewer: OK, tell me a little bit about yourself, Marina.
Marina: Sure. My name's Marina Kennedy. I'm 36. I live in Atlanta, Georgia, and I work for a large insurance company. I'm an executive in the sales department. Uh, let's see . . . I'm single. I have my own apartment . . .
Interviewer: Do you like living alone?
Marina: Mmmm . . . yes, . . . I get lonely sometimes, but I like having my privacy, too.

INTERVIEW 2

Interviewer: So, Bob, you study at Northwestern?
Bob: No, at the University of Southern Illinois. I'm majoring in psychology.
Interviewer: And you work, too?
Bob: I work at night, in a bookstore, down at the Riverside shopping mall.
Interviewer: Do you live with your family, Bob?
Bob: No, I live with a roommate. We have an apartment near the university. But . . . I don't know . . .
Interviewer: You don't like living with a roommate?
Bob: Well, not *this* roommate. He's kind of crazy.

INTERVIEW 3

Interviewer: Could you tell me a little bit about yourself, Mr. Henderson?
Henderson: Well, I'm vice president of a large company here in New York—Beacon Industries. We have factories all over the country, but our main office is here in New York.
Interviewer: And what about your family?
Henderson: I'm married, I have two children, and we live here in Manhattan.
Interviewer: Do you like your work?
Henderson: Yes, very much. It takes a lot of my time—I'm always busy—but I enjoy it.

INTERVIEW 4

Ted: My name is Ted Small. I'm a math teacher. I know, everybody hates math, right? But I really like teaching math, especially to young children.
Interviewer: Are you married, Mr. Small?
Ted: You can call me Ted. I'm a widower. My wife died five years ago—so I live alone now—but I'm very busy. My daughter and her children come to visit me a lot, and I'm very busy helping my students.

Chapter 1, Page 3, Input

I really enjoy being a realtor because . . . well, I like meeting people. When someone buys a house—it's a very important decision—and I like being involved. I like helping people, especially young people who are looking for their first house. We have to work very hard—we often work on the weekends and we don't have a lot of free time. But it's funny—some days we work, oh, twelve hours a day, driving all over the city showing houses. And then there are days when there's no work at all—nothing really to do—and I just sit at my desk and wait for the phone to ring. Let's see, what else? My job pays well. And . . . I don't know . . . I like my job. It's interesting—and I think I'm pretty good at it, too!

Chapter 2, Page 9, Presentation

CONVERSATION 1

A: Excuse me, when's the next train to Oxford?
B: At 3:17.
A: Are there any trains after that?
B: There's one at 3:30 and another one at 4:12 and . . .
A: The 4:12 is fine. Do I have to change anywhere?
B: No, it's direct.
A: What time does it get into Oxford?
B: At 5:18.
A: And . . . how much is that . . . round trip?
B: Eight pounds fifty, sir. Platform 5.

CONVERSATION 2

A: I'm sorry to bother you, but does this bus stop near the Metropolitan Museum of Art?
B: The museum?
A: Yes, the museum.
B: Well, you get on and ask the bus driver for a transfer. Then you get off at Madison Avenue and take the uptown bus. Then you get off at 82nd Street and walk one block west.
A: Thanks. Do I need exact change for the bus?
B: Uh-huh, you do. Here it comes. I'm taking this bus too, so I can tell you when we get to Madison.
A: Thanks a lot. I appreciate it.

CONVERSATION 3

A: Uh, est-ce que vous . . . uh . . .
B: Would you like to speak English?
A: Oh, yes. When is the next bus to Ottawa, and how much is it?
B: Is that round trip or one way?
A: One way, please.
B: It's 35 dollars, please.
A: When does the next bus leave?
B: Well, it leaves in two minutes, sir.

A: Two minutes! Could you hurry, please? Do you take American Express? What about my baggage?
B: Je suis desolé, Monsieur. There it goes.
A: Stop that bus! I mean "bus." Arrête!

CONVERSATION 4

George: I'll ask this man, Marjorie.
Marjorie: All right.
George: Excuse me, I'm looking for Taft Street.
Stranger: Sorry, I'm a stranger here myself.
George: Oh, that's OK. Thank you anyway.
Marjorie: I'm going to ask this man. Excuse me, we're looking for Taft Street.
Foreigner: Perdão, mas não falo ingles . . .
George: We need some answers. Oh, excuse me, sir, I'm looking for Taft Street . . .
Man: Ah!
George: Now we'll get some answers.
Man: Ranff Sweenfw! Moo yusnf ro rownf a fewf serfw nuumf.
George: OK. Thank you. And what's a good place to eat around here? You know—not too expensive.
Man: Fvwell, moo fn fwoo ua vwittuh . . .
George: Thank you *very* much. One more question—where can I cash some traveler's checks around here?
Man: Fwavwuhs fweckf? Vwfell, twown vuh fweet vef a pfwafe feh . . .
George: Thank you. You've been very helpful.
Marjorie: George, I couldn't understand a word that man said.
George: I couldn't either, but at least we got some *answers!*

Chapter 2, Page 10, Input

Frank: There's the bus stop.
Liz: Oh, good.
Frank: Excuse me, does this bus go to Napoleon's Tomb?
Stranger: Yes, it does.
Frank and Liz: Thanks.
Stranger: Here it comes now.
Frank: Uh, how much is it to Napoleon's Tomb?
Driver: Les Invalides? Deux francs—two francs, please.
Liz: Ask him to tell us . . .
Frank: Uh, could you tell us when we get there?
Driver: Oui, oui.
Driver: Les Invalides.
Frank and Liz: Thanks./Thank you.
Liz: I don't see it. It's a big building, isn't it?
Frank: Yeah, let's walk down this way.
Liz: It's almost lunchtime. Why don't we get something to eat before we go? Ask that man if there's a good place to eat around here.
Frank: Uh, excuse me, do you speak English?
Man: Yes, a little.
Frank: We're looking for a restaurant—not too expensive—but one that has good food.
Man: Yes, the Café des Invalides is just down the street.
Frank and Liz: Thank you./Thank you very much.
Liz: Oh, I have to mail these postcards. Ask that lady if there's a post office near here.
Frank: OK. Excuse me, madam, where's the nearest post office?
Lady: Dans la Rue de la Concorde.
Frank: Thank you very much. Let's get organized and find Napoleon's Tomb. Isn't that why we're here?
Liz: OK. Ask that policeman over there.
Frank: You go and ask him.
Liz: Sure. I'll ask him—and *I'll* do it in French. Watch this. Uh, . . . uh, . . . excusez-moi, uh . . . monsieur, uh . . . je . . . je . . . uh je cherche . . . uh . . . je cherche Napoleon.
Gendarme: Napoleon? Napoleon Bonaparte?
Liz: Oui.
Gendarme: Mais, Madame, il est mort. He is dead, Madame.

Chapter 3, Page 16, Presentation

COUNTRY 1

This country borders the United States and is famous for its ancient Indian civilizations—the Mayas, the Toltecs, and the Aztecs. It is an agricultural country that grows cotton, sugarcane, and coffee. Its capital is the largest city in the world, with a population of over 15 million. This country also produces steel, chemicals, and oil.

COUNTRY 2

This country is made up of four islands in eastern Asia. It is small in size but has a population of almost 120 million. It is an industrial nation that manufactures cars and electronic equipment. It is famous for its beautiful scenery, including its many mountains and volcanoes and its spectacular waterfalls.

COUNTRY 3

Many people say that democracy and Western culture had their beginnings in this country. The mainland is situated in southern Europe on the Mediterranean Sea. Among more than 2,000 small islands that are also a part of this country are Corfu and Crete. This beautiful country attracts a lot of tourists each year who like the sunny weather and the warm Mediterranean beaches. This country is a member of the Common Market. It also belongs to NATO.

Chapter 3, Page 19, Input

Mike: You're from Canada, aren't you, Karen?
Karen: That's right.
Mike: So you speak French, too, right?
Karen: Well, not really. I speak a little French—I learned it in school—but I'm from Ontario, and it's basically an English-speaking province.
Mike: Oh, that's right. It's in Quebec that they speak French.
Karen: Yeah.
Mike: So how many people speak French in Canada, anyway?
Karen: As a first language, about 25 percent, but a lot of people are bilingual.
Mike: What's the population of Canada? It's bigger than the U.S., isn't it?
Karen: Yes, in size it's very large—the second largest country in the world—but our population is only 25 million, not very many people for such an enormous country.
Mike: And your capital—the capital of Canada—is Toronto, isn't it?
Karen: No, Toronto is the largest city in Canada, but it isn't the capital. Ottawa is.
Mike: My first impression when I think about Canada is that it's a very cold country with a lot of snow.
Karen: Well, it is true that our climate is difficult, but we have warm—sometimes hot—weather in the summer. The winters are very long and cold. Minus 20 degrees Celsius is a normal temperature for the winter.
Mike: Minus 20? That's *cold!* If I ever come to visit you, it will be in August.

Chapter 4, Page 24, Presentation

CONVERSATION 1

A: Hi, can I help you?
B: Could you tell me the price of this squash racket, please?
A: Uh-huh. It's $65.50.
B: Hmmm, I didn't really want to spend that much. How much are those jogging shorts?
A: $10.98.
B: Could I try them on?
A: Sure. Over there.

CONVERSATION 2

A: How does it feel ?
B: Uh, do you have it in a larger size, a 12, maybe?
A: I think so. Let me check.
B: And do you have it in dark blue?
A: Let me go and check for you.

CONVERSATION 3

A: May I help you, sir?
B: Uh, I'm just looking for now, thanks.
A: Fine. If you need any help . . .
B: Could I see that CD player, please?
A: Sure. We just got these in. They sound great—and there's a 15 percent discount, too.
B: Oh! Do you sell the compact discs, too?
A: No, you can get them at the record shop next door.

CONVERSATION 4

A: Good evening. Are you ready to order?
B: Yes, we'll have the lobster special, please.
A: What would you like to drink?
B: We'll have some white wine, please. And could you bring us an ashtray?
A: I'm afraid you're not in the smoking section. Would you like to move?
B: No, we'll stay here.

Chapter 4, Page 27, Input

Ms. Stacey: Hi. Can I help you with something?
Paul: I'm looking for . . . uh, well, . . . I don't know what I'm looking for, really. It's my mother's birthday tomorrow and, uh, . . .
Ms. Stacey: Well, what about clothes? Maybe she'd like a nice blouse. . . like this.
Paul: That's really nice.
Ms. Stacey: What's your mother's size?
Paul: I don't know. I don't know what size she takes.
Ms. Stacey: That's a problem. Does your mother like perfume or makeup?
Paul: Well, I don't think she wears makeup very much, and she already has a lot of perfume. How much are those earrings over there?
Ms. Stacey: Let's go and see. They're 40 dollars.
Paul: Oh, I didn't want to spend that much.
Ms. Stacey: How about a pocket calculator? They're not very expensive.
Paul: She already has a calculator.
Ms. Stacey: Well, what do you think your mother would really like?
Paul: Oh, she'd *love* a video camera, but I can't afford that . . . Uh, thanks a lot. Sorry to bother you. I'll just keep looking.

(ONE HOUR LATER)

Ms. Stacey: So, did you find anything for your mother?
Paul: Yeah! I got a five-pound box of cookies, a pair of Adidas socks, and a new rock album, really cheap.
Ms. Stacey: Are you sure she's going to like all those things?
Paul: Why not?

Ms. Stacey: And if she doesn't, *you* can always use them, right?
Paul: Hey, yeah, that's right. Well, bye and thanks.
Ms. Stacey: Kids!

Chapter 5, Page 33, Presentation

Speaker 1: Well, one thing I remember very clearly . . . was when we moved from a really small town to a big city. I was only 6 years old at the time and it was a real shock.
Speaker 2: It was . . . when my sister was born. Finally I had somebody to play with—and to fight with, too.
Speaker 3: It was just three months ago when I finally passed a math test.
Speaker 4: Oh, when I had my son! My husband and I were both 40 years old, and we were so happy that we finally had a baby.
Speaker 5: When I met my wife.
Speaker 6: Oh, the first day I went to school. I was so scared.
Speaker 7: I remember when I smoked my first cigarette. A friend of mine had a pack of Winstons and we went into the boys' bathroom at school. It was . . . ugh . . . I never smoked again.
Speaker 8: Three things that I remember all sort of happened together. I won a prize for a poem I wrote at school—then I graduated from high school that same month—and after that I went to Brandeis University.

Chapter 5, Page 34, Input

October 16, 1986: The 1986 Nobel Prize for Literature was awarded today to the Nigerian writer Wole Soyinka.

Soyinka was born in 1934 in a village near the Nigerian city of Ibadan. He first went to college in Ibadan. Later he went to England to attend the University of Leeds and graduated in 1958. Some of his early plays were then performed in London.

In 1960 Soyinka returned to Nigeria. That year his country gained its independence from British rule. During this time he wrote such well-known works as *A Dance of the Forests* and *Kongi's Harvest.* He also edited a magazine and organized a national theater.

In his writings Soyinka praised Nigerian independence. However, he also attacked the government when he thought that it did not respect the goals of that independence. In 1967 he was arrested by the Nigerian government and spent almost two years in prison. Wole Soyinka is a hero in his country and respected internationally as a brilliant writer.

Chapter 6, Page 39, Presentation

Ellen: Well, I get up at six o'clock every day. I have to be at the studio before seven—for them to work on my hair, makeup, things like that. I always take time to have a big breakfast before I leave the house . . . eggs, cereal, juice . . . a big breakfast. I find that I really need the energy. When possible, I walk to the studio. But if I get up a little late or if it's raining, I drive. I usually start work around eight. There's a cafeteria at the studio, so I usually eat lunch there. I have a really long day . . . most of the time. Sometimes I don't go home until nine o'clock at night. But then the weekend comes—ahhhh. I like to spend the weekends with my family and just relax. I don't even think about work.
Kevin: I get up at eight, usually make myself a fast cup of coffee, and drive to my office. I have a big, bright red car with a great stereo. I get to work around nine. Sometimes I have to drive out to a construction site and stay there most of the day. I have lunch at a restaurant and then at five o'clock I'm in my car and on my way home. At night I usually watch TV. The problem with my job is that I often have to work on the weekends—Saturday especially. Oh, well, I can't complain.

Chapter 6, Page 41, Input

Paula: So, who are you going out with tonight, Clara?
Clara: I can't decide.
Paula: What about Mike?
Clara: No, I don't think so. All Mike talks about is career, career, career. He works at night. He works all *weekend.* And Tony . . . Tony goes to Art School three times a week and wants me to go with him. He paints on the weekend. I'm not into that.
Paula: You could go out with Dave.
Clara: Why? Dave spends Saturday jogging and playing tennis. He *really* likes sports and I don't.
Paula: What about John? You like John.
Clara: Yeah, John makes me laugh. What a sense of humor! He tells jokes all the time, but I don't want to go out with him tonight.
Paula: Why don't you go out with Jack?
Clara: Jack! Go *out* with Jack? Jack sits home and watches TV all night. A person doesn't go *out* with Jack.
Paula: Frank?
Clara: Frank talks too much. He goes to a classical music concert or an art exhibit practically every night. In his free time he writes poetry. I want to have fun.
Paula: Well, then, stay home.
Clara: Yeah, I think I will. It's terrible when you have no one to go out with.
Paula: Yeah, I know.

Chapter 7, Page 48, Presentation

CONVERSATION 1

Sylvia: David, have you met Caroline?
David: Caroline! How've you been?
Caroline: Great, David! It's good to see you again. How are you—and how's your sister?
David: Oh, she's fine. She's working now, you know.
Caroline: Is she still going to school?
David: Yeah, she's studying at night and working during the day.
Caroline: Oh, she must be busy. Is she still studying at New York University?

CONVERSATION 2

Sylvia: Caroline, this is my cousin, Bennett, who works at NBC. Oh, excuse me for a second . . .
Caroline: Nice to meet you, Bennett.
Bennett: Nice to meet you, too.
Caroline: How long have you been at NBC?
Bennett: Only a year and a half. Sylvia tells me you work there too. How long have you been there?
Caroline: About a year and a half, too.
Bennett: That's funny. I never see you around. Where do you work?
Caroline: In the personnel department.
Bennett: Oh, *that's* why. That's on the third floor.

CONVERSATION 3

David: I don't believe it. Bennett Grace!
Bennett: Well, I'll be! David Larsen. How've you been? It's great to see you again. How long have you been in New York?
David: Oh, five years now.
Bennett: I just don't believe it. How's Barbara?
David: Well, we're divorced now.
Bennett: Oh, I'm sorry.
David: But she's fine. She's living in New Jersey now, working at a library there. How's your family? What's Vanessa doing these days?
Bennett: Oh, she's studying hard, as usual—taking painting lessons, ballet, computer classes.

CONVERSATION 4

Sylvia: Sulie, do you know my cousin, Bennett?
Sulie: No, nice to meet you, Bennett.
Bennett: Nice to meet you, too.
Sylvia: Sulie's from Brazil, Bennett. Oh, excuse me for a minute, will you?
Bennett: From Brazil. Wow! How long have you been here?
Sulie: For three months.
Bennett: How do you like it here?
Sulie: Well, it's different . . .
Bennett: Are you on vacation?
Sulie: No, actually, I'm studying at Pratt Institute. I . . .

Chapter 7, Page 50, Input

Stranger: Well, it's George Carson. How've you been, you old devil?
George: Oh, uh, good, good! Uh . . . How are *you*, . . . uh . . .
Stranger: Oh, just fine. I can't believe it. You look great. Maybe a little less hair . . . and a little more stomach, but, you know, I'd recognize you anywhere.
George: Yeah, well, we're all getting older, uh . . .
Stranger: And how's Doris?
George: Oh, she's fine. Uh, she's right over there. Doris, could you come over here? You remember our old friend, uh . . . uh . . .
Stranger: Doris, you look as beautiful as ever. I can't believe it, I really can't!
Doris: Oh, and how are you? It's so good to see you again.
Stranger: Just fine. Are you still living in Port Findlay?
Doris and George: Yes, we are. We're still there.
Stranger: And how about the kids? What's Mike doing these days?
George: Uh, he's in Toronto—he's been there, oh, five years now.
Doris: Yes, he's married now and he's teaching high school in Toronto.
Stranger: Oh, that's great. Is Marli still working at that bookstore?
Doris: No, she's back at school, working on her Master's. Uh, how's your family?
Stranger: Oh, they're all fine. Marion is living in New York now, and of course Kathy's been in Florida for almost ten years now.
Doris and George: Oh, that's nice. Very nice, uh . . .
Stranger: Well, I can't tell you how great it is to see you two again, yes sir.
Doris: It was very nice seeing you, too.
George: Uh, yes, very nice seeing you again . . . uh . . .
Stranger: Take care now. Say hi to the kids.
Doris and George: Yes. Sure. We will.
George: OK. Who *is* he?
Doris: *I* don't know. I thought *you* did.
George: No. I never saw him before.
Doris: Well, I don't know who he is.
George: I'm sure I never saw him before in my life!

Chapter 8, Page 56, Presentation

CONVERSATION 1

Marlene: So, Julie, how was Rio?
Julie: Oh, we had a *great* time, Marlene. We stayed at a really nice little hotel—right on Copacabana beach. It was wonderful.

Marlene: So you really liked it, huh? What did you do?
Julie: Well, we went sightseeing almost every day. It's a beautiful city. The people were really friendly, too—and the food was great!
Marlene: Did you do much shopping?
Julie: Yeah, we bought a few things—some clothes and souvenirs. We drank *lots* of coffee. Their coffee is so good.

CONVERSATION 2

A: I called your house last night, but you weren't home.
B: No, I went out with Paul and a friend of his from San Francisco.
A: Yeah?
B: Yeah, we took him out for dinner at Zack's—that new restaurant on Summit Street.
A: Oh yeah. Was it OK?
B: I was disappointed. The food was nothing special—and it was really expensive.
A: Oh, too bad.
B: We went to a nightclub after dinner.
A: That's good.

CONVERSATION 3

A: Do you like my new coat?
B: Ooh! Let me see. Oh, it's great! Where did you get it?
A: I bought it at Burberry's—on sale. It wasn't expensive at all.
B: That's a good store. They have a lot of nice things.
A: Yeah, but I didn't like the salesperson who waited on me. She wasn't very nice.
B: Oh.

Chapter 8, Page 58, Input

PART ONE

Mark: Yeah, I had a pretty interesting day yesterday. It was a good day. First of all, I went downtown and . . . I met someone . . . at around 9 o'clock . . . and we went to talk to a man about an ad in the newspaper. Then I went to the bank because I didn't have very much money and I had to buy something . . . expensive. So . . . I bought what I needed and then we had lunch—my friend and I. We went to a really expensive restaurant . . . to celebrate. I paid, and it was a fortune. Then later on I went to the movies—but I left before it was over. I went home after that. And then I went to bed early because it was important for me to get up early in the morning.

PART TWO

Girl: Come on, Mark. How about some more information about your day?
Mark: OK, OK. I met a friend of mine downtown. I had an appointment to see a man about a job that was in the newspaper, and my friend came along to keep me company. OK, so I talked to this man, Mr. Baker, and do you believe it? I got the job.
Girl: Great, Mark.
Mark: The new job is going to involve a lot of work with computers, so I got some money out of the bank and bought myself a personal computer to use at home. Boy, it was *really* expensive. Then I took my friend out to lunch at a French restaurant to celebrate my new job. I paid sixty bucks for the two of us—which I thought was pretty expensive. Let's see. Later I went to the movies. It was a horror movie—terrible, just terrible—so I left before it was over. Then I went home. I went to bed early because I didn't want to be late for my first day of work, right? There. Are you satisfied?
Girl: Yes. That's much better.

Chapter 9, Page 64, Presentation

Kim: Well, I'm going to be an actress. When I finish school, I'm going straight to Hollywood. First I'm going to become a model. After that, I might sign a contract with MGM—or maybe with Columbia. It depends on who offers me more money. Oh yes, I'm going to live in Beverly Hills, too.
Charles: Well, my father has my life all planned. I'm going to finish school and then I'm going to work for his company. He says he's going to make me vice president. He's probably going to decide when I get married and who I'm going to marry and where I'm going to live and how many children. . . .
Dave: When I finish school, I'm going to ask my uncle to lend me some money. You can make a *fortune* with just a little money. I have a friend who's a genius at fixing motors and things—so we're going to buy old motorcycles, fix them up, and sell them. Then we're going to take the money we make and open up a repair shop—and make a lot of money. After that I might start an avocado farm in California—or I might go up north and look for gold—I've got a lot of ideas!

Chapter 9, Page 66, Input

Daniel: Well, I'm going to graduate next year. I might go back to my hometown, or I might specialize first—I'm not sure yet. But I'm planning to work in the small village where I was born, helping the people there. That's really important to me—that's the reason I became a doctor. I'd like to start a children's clinic some day—or a hospital for old people.
Ken: Um, I'm planning to get married next year. My fiancé and I are both psychologists, and we're going to work in the inner city with teenagers. I'd like to work in the high schools, maybe. My fiancé already has a job. She starts next month. She's going to work in a clinic.

Tina: I'm a teacher at a public school in my country. But I'm not going to teach in the public school system next year. There are a lot of adults in my country who can't read or write. Next year I'm planning to join a group of teachers and we're going to begin a literacy program for adults in rural areas. . . .

Mario: I'm going to get my degree in agricultural engineering next year. After that I'm planning to get my master's. When I finish school, I'd like to work for the Ministry of Agriculture. I'd really like to go into the country and help farmers—teach them new technology.

Jayah: I started a business last year. We make electronic equipment and the business is really doing well—so I'm planning to hire more people. My country has a big program for the handicapped and I'd like to help. I'm going to adapt some of the equipment for the handicapped, and I'm hoping that the government will help us with a loan. . . .

Chapter 10, Page 73, Presentation

CONVERSATION 1

Woman: If you think we're going to buy you a motorcycle, then you're crazy!

Boy: But why not? Dad says I can't have a car, so why can't I have a motorcycle? They're a lot cheaper.

Woman: And a lot more dangerous.

Boy: Mom, lots of guys I know have motorcyles. They're great! They're much easier to park than a car, you don't spend as much on gas . . . and in city traffic they're a lot faster . . .

Woman: Ah ha!

CONVERSATION 2

Wife: Let's get a pet. How about a cat?

Husband: Well, to tell you the truth, I'd really rather have a dog.

Wife: Why? Cats are so cute and they're cleaner than dogs.

Husband: But dogs are friendlier, easier to train, and more obedient.

Wife: Maybe, but cats are quieter. They don't bark. They're also more intelligent.

Husband: I heard that *dogs* were more intelligent.

Wife: OK. I can see we're never going to agree. Why don't we get a parakeet?

CONVERSATION 3

Woman 1: I know a good opera that we can go see this weekend at the Metropolitan.

Woman 2: An opera? I'd rather go to a rock concert. The Bubbles are playing at a club downtown on Saturday night.

Woman 1: Oh no. A rock concert is so much noisier and more crowded than an opera. I don't like that.

Woman 2: But a rock concert is more exciting and the club downtown is easier to get to than the Metropolitan.

Woman 1: Well, OK. But next weekend we go to the opera.

Woman 2: OK. It's a deal.

Chapter 10, Page 74, Input

Psychiatrist: Would you like to lie down on the couch, Kathy?

Kathy: I think so, Dr. Marley.

Psychiatrist: Why don't we talk some more about your sister? We didn't get a chance to finish that last week. So let's continue.

Kathy: Well, like I said last week, I've always had an inferiority complex because of Julie. *She* was always the pretty one . . . really pretty . . . slim . . . tall . . . graceful, like a model. You know, a really funny and happy person, too.

Psychiatrist: Uh-huh.

Kathy: She always got better grades in school, too. You know, she has a 150 IQ. Mine's 125.

Psychiatrist: Tell me, how old is Julie?

Kathy: Five years older than me. You know, my mother always used to say, "Look how neat and clean Julie is . . . and how talented" . . . and on and on and . . .

Psychiatrist: How did you feel about that?

Kathy: It really bothered me. It really did.

Psychiatrist: What about now? Where's Julie now?

Kathy: In Federal Prison for fraud . . .

Psychiatrist: Oh, really!

Kathy: Writing bad checks. That was always my best quality . . . *I* was the honest one.